1978

The Theatre
of
ORSON WELLES

The Theatre
of
ORSON WELLES

Richard France

Lewisburg
Bucknell University Press
London: Associated University Presses

Associated University Presses, Inc.
Cranbury, New Jersey 08512

Associated University Presses
Magdalen House
136-148 Tooley Street
London SE1 2TT, England

Library of Congress Cataloging in Publication Data

France, Richard, 1938-
    The theatre of Orson Welles.

    Bibliography: p.
    Includes index.
    1. Welles, Orson, 1915-   2. Theatrical
producers and directors—United States—Biography.
I. Title.
PN2287.W456F7   792'.0233'0924 [B]   76-14767
ISBN 0-8387-1972-4

PRINTED IN THE UNITED STATES OF AMERICA

for
Nellie S. Mehr
and the memory of
Joseph L. Mehr

Contents

FOREWORD by Robert W. Corrigan   9
PREFACE   13
ACKNOWLEDGMENTS   17

1   Early Welles: 1931-36   21
2   The "Voodoo" *Macbeth* (Lafayette Theater, New York,
    April 14, 1936)   54
3   *Horse Eats Hat* (Maxine Elliott Theater, New York,
    September 26, 1936)   74
4   *Doctor Faustus* (Maxine Elliott Theater, New York,
    January 8, 1937)   88
5   *The Cradle Will Rock*: A Comment (Venice Theater, New York,
    June 16, 1937)   97
6   *Julius Caesar* (Mercury Theatre, New York,
    November 11, 1937)   106
7   *The Shoemaker's Holiday* (Mercury Theatre, New York,
    January 1, 1938)   124
8   *Danton's Death* (Mercury Theatre, New York,
    November 2, 1938)   142
9   *Five Kings* (Colonial Theater, Boston, February 27, 1938)   155
10   The Radio Years: 1934-40   171

APPENDIX A: Cast Lists of the Stage Productions   181
APPENDIX B: Selected Radio Credits   191
NOTES   193
BIBLIOGRAPHY   196
INDEX   209

Foreword

After reading Richard France's interesting and illuminating account of Orson Welles's relatively short but tempestuous career in the theatre, I couldn't help but come to the conclusion that Welles's work seems to have embodied the theory and practice of nearly all of the modern theatre's most innovative and seminal directors. He had the encompassing and essentially fascistic vision of a Wagner. His aspiration to achieve a unified art of the theatre, not to mention his treatment of actors as marionettes, is reminiscent of Gordon Craig. From all accounts, he directed crowd scenes with the meticulous concern for detail that we associate with Ludwig Kranek and his Meininger Company. He used boldly expressionistic staging techniques that would rival those of Leopold Jessner. His ideas about the role of lighting in a production reminds one of Appia. His almost cavalier willingness to alter scripts to serve his own purposes followed the practice of Meyerhold and, more recently, Grotowski. He organized each production in the manner of Max Reinhardt, and yet his rehearsals seem to have been imbued with the spirit of improvization that we associate with such contemporary experimentalists as Chaikin, Schechner, and the Becks. And finally, his populist view of the theatre's primary purpose was in accord with those of Brecht — or at least those propounded by Brecht in the 1920s. In short, almost every tendency of modern stagecraft seems to have coalesced in the work of the then *enfant terrible* of the American Theatre. However, in saying this, one thing must be made clearly understood: There was nothing studied or academic about him or his work. He didn't have *Directors on Directing* in his library, he never had a course in "Contemporary Trends in the Theatre," nor did he do graduate work in directing (he, in fact, never went to college.) Orson Welles seems to be almost parthenogenetic. Everything he did sprang from his singular and uniquely committed vision of the theatre. This is the central clue to all of his work.

The one thing that comes through most forcefully in Professor France's book is the fact that no matter what project Welles embarked on, he was much more interested in his *own* response to the work than he was in making manifest the mysteries and meanings that resided in the work itself. Now this can be a tricky and dangerous business. We know what a mixed bag one gets when we make Shakespeare our contemporary; for every interesting and more or less successful "Beckettized" *King Lear,* we get such abominations as "Puck on Roller Skates," *Love's Labours Lost* in psychedelic drag, or a rock version of *Hamlet.* Whenever a director seeks to "translate" the world of a play into what he thinks are terms appropriate for his audience, he is actually being much more a critic than an artist. The theatre doesn't need translating, for this always occurs when the imaginative figures of the play are transformed into presences by the actors. I am convinced that the theatre exists — and always has — to make manifest life's mysteries and that audiences go to the theatre because of a need to make contact with and share in these realms. The function of theatre is not demystification but the presentation of strangeness. Criticism, on the other hand, exists to help us find a common ground between the audience and that which is made manifest in the theatre. If the theatre assumes the critical task of alleviating strangeness, where are we to go for the experience of the mystery itself? I am sure that Ionesco had something like this in mind when he wrote, "I've raised a whole flock of demystifiers for you. They'll demystify you. But to demystify, you must first mystify. We need a new mystification," and that is why so much of our theatre presents us with little more than the maimed rites of aborted ceremony. Welles always ran the risk of doing this in his work, and Professor France's study indicates that at times he, in fact, did. But finally, his innate sense of artistic rightness transcended both the limitations of his response and his tendency to overconceptualize. Thank God, the always powerful and often anarchic Rabelaisian spirit of Welles the artist ultimately asserted itself.

Welles the artist — how best to describe him? All of his work is marked by excess — an excess carried almost to the point of baroque amplification. But to say this is to oversimplify and be misleading. I said earlier that Welles had a very special vision of the theatre (and the film, as well), and Professor France gives us a most significant adumbration of this vision when he points out that in attempting to create a popular theatre, Welles was governed not by a tragic view of life, but rather the vision of a comic melodramatist. This is a Falstaffian vision, a vision of infinite possibility, a combination of infantile excess, innocent self-importance, ironic self-knowledge, and the constant need for attention. I am convinced that it is no accident that Welles's most ambitious character was Falstaff of his last theatre piece, *Five Kings,* and I further believe that all of his major film roles are, in fact, variants of Prince Hal's "Dog beneath the skin." Probably the supreme embodiment of this vision in the modern theatre was George Bernard Shaw, and, despite obvious external differences, I find striking similarities between Orson Welles and GBS. One recalls the time when Granville-Barker was having difficulty with his production of *Androcles and the Lion* and Shaw gave him this advice: "Remember that it's Italian opera." He could have been speaking of the grandiose and excessive theatrical style of everything Welles has done. (In this regard, I believe that W. H. Auden's comment on Falstaff is also pertinent: "Falstaff belongs to the *opera buffe* world of play and mock action. . . .The essential Falstaff is the Falstaff of *The Merry Wives* and Verdi's opera, the comic hero of the world of play.")

Both Shaw and Welles understood melodrama's strong hold on the popular imagination. Both realized that melodrama's greatest achievement is its capacity to give direct objective form to our most savage superstitions, our most neurotic fantasies, and our most grotesque childhood imaginings. And yet the dominant tone of paranoia that characterizes most melodrama — a tone that is often enhanced by wild and threatening scenic effects and emotionally excessive music — is leavened in the work of Shaw and Welles by an equally powerful comic sense of life. It is this combination that makes them unique in the modern theatre. It is also the combination that produced Welles's finest work, *Citizen Kane,* which is often referred to as one of the great comic melodramas of the twentieth century.

Today we think of Orson Welles almost entirely in terms of his achievements in film. We can all be grateful to Richard France for tracing his earlier career in the theatre, for it is clear that his work in theatre was more than an apprenticeship. Welles is a creative link between these two worlds, and if *Citizen Kane* brought a new maturity to the film, it is a maturity that is rooted in the rich tradition of the modern stage.

Robert W. Corrigan

Preface

It has been suggested that Orson Welles set out "to make a total and universal demonstration of the possibilities of cinema," that he felt some internal need "to assemble and mold those multiple personalities, scattered and contradictory, that one by one had thrown him into the theatre, radio and television (not to mention art, music, politics, vaudeville, ballet, ad infinitum) and threatened to overwhelm him altogether at any moment". *Citizen Kane* is characterized as being "first and foremost an attempt to assemble the pieces of the Wellesian mosaic, a formidable, unifying projection of his multiple personalities."[1]

Remarks of this sort, only too common in dealing with his films, are revealing mainly because they suggest a kind of artistic and personal schizophrenia in Welles himself. It is as if his work in the various media all existed as separate entities in need of some catalytic element. In fact, Welles's development was continuous and remarkably consistent. Whether in film, radio, or the theatre, Welles exhibited the same artistic tendencies. Thus, *Citizen Kane* was not a unique phenomenon in the total Welles oeuvre, but rather a stage in his development as an artist.

This study will concentrate on his work in the theatre, which not only represents a unique and innovative creative achievement in itself but also provides significant insight for an understanding of his films.

Charles Higham, groping for the essence of Welles's film art, suggests that it must lie in some profound statement about *life*.

> His masterpieces confront dissolution with shows of energy. . . .A black and driving obsession with dissolution and an addiction to the pleasures of the flesh are the two sides of the hedonism that Welles has embraced.[2]

He understands Welles's use of structure as a means of revealing some ultimate content, specifically autobiographical. Each film that Welles has failed to complete is seen as another attempt to ward off approaching dissolution. In Higham's search for the profundities of Welles's art, he has formulated a kind of psychohistorical pattern into which he attempts to squeeze the films. This pattern is not only misleading, it is beside the point. In confusing Welles the man with his work,

13

Higham completely fails to recognize the nature of that work, and he is led to the outrageous conclusion that Welles did not understand or find a mass audience.

Pauline Kael, on the other hand, speaks of *Citizen Kane* in quite different terms. To her it is indeed a masterpiece, albeit a shallow masterpiece. The lack of depth is attributed to the fact that *Kane* was intended as popular entertainment. Throughout Welles's career as a stage director, critics often praised the profundity of his theatrical concepts; yet, like *Kane* they too were conceived with an eye toward audience appeal. Profundity has never been the source of Welles's greatness.

In *Kane* he utilized the durable and popular format of melodrama, made relevant by the addition of Freud and scandal. Kael is not the least bit disturbed that the result was a "comic strip" about Hearst. Quite the contrary. She admires Welles's unique and daring manipulation of the formal elements of the film whereby he was able to give aesthetic credibility to content that can only be described as "kitsch".

In comparing Higham and Kael's criticisms, one is struck by the fact that, unburdened by the need to find (to force, really) a thematic pattern on it, she actually *saw* the film. Andrew Sarris, in analyzing its thematic structure, pointed out three serious faults in *Citizen Kane*: "(1) its narrative structure is unduly complicated; (2) its technique calls attention to itself; (3) its intellectual content is superficial."[3]

It is precisely these "faults" that are, in fact, Welles's chief merits. The uniqueness of a Welles production is that its form, not its content, carries his meaning. What Kael found so remarkable about the movies was true of all of his work.

A great deal of Welles criticism, both favorable and unfavorable, has really been directed toward those tendencies in art which are characteristically "modern"—one critic railing against Welles's lack of drama, the other decorating his remarks with notions about theme and the development of ideas. Both camps, however, are suspicious if not openly hostile to the instincts and sensibilities that Welles, though largely unaware of it, shared with the European avant-garde of his day.

In his work in the theatre, Welles grasped this central insight into the relationship between form and content. The specific meaning of a Welles production was contained in its very form, with the objective content serving to amplify this meaning and make a rhetorical understanding of it readily available. He utilized many of the forms and techniques of expressionist drama. Walter Sokel tells us that "Expressionism, as abstract form, as part of the modernist movement, and Expressionism as a formless shriek, arise from the same factor—subjectivism".[4] In Welles's work subjectivism meant that dramatic experience was revealed through formal structure on the one hand, and almost "tactile" theatricality on the other, rather than through the ostensible rhetoric of his scripts.

Two of Welles's productions have been deliberately omitted from this study: *Too Much Johnson,* because it was an abortive production; and *Heartbreak House,* because Welles was forced to adhere to the original text ("NO CUTS!" G.B.S."), and it resulted in a conventional Broadway production.

Likewise, no attempt has been made to reconstruct *The Cradle Will Rock*; its final form was purely accidental, and that accident has been described in countless anecdotes, biographies, and histories of the theatre — notably, John Houseman's splendid book of memoirs, *Run-Through.* But a comment on how this accident was manipulated to further Houseman and Welles's plans to gain support for their own theatre is long overdue.

Acknowledgements

The idea and format for this study originated with Professor Leon Katz of Carnegie-Mellon University. Its final version owes its existence to my wife, Rachel, and to Professor Henry Sellin of New York University. To them and to Professor Earle Gister of the City University of New York I wish to acknowledge my most profound gratitude.

A debt of gratitude is also due to Samuel Leve, Edwin Denby, James Morcom, and Walter Ash, for the use of their manuscripts, ground plans, renderings, and photographs; to Edna Thomas for making me a present of Welles's original rehearsal notes for the "Voodoo" *Macbeth;* to Virgil Thomson for his sage council, his referrals, and for allowing me to examine his and Paul Bowles's musical scores for *Macbeth* and *Horse Eats Hat* respectively; to Richard Wilson for opening his set of Mercury files to me; to John Houseman for granting the necessary permissions to reproduce and to quote from such WPA and Mercury production books as are still available; to Arnold Weissberger for his continued efforts to put me in direct contact with Welles; to Rupert Loughlin and the Irish National Library for documenting Welles's activities in Dublin; to Kay Johnson and the Wisconsin Center for Theatre Research for the copy of *Brite Lucifer;* to Paul Myers and the Theatre Collection of the Library and Museum of the Performing Arts at Lincoln Center; to Dean Thomas Headrick and the Lawrence University Faculty Research Fund; to James Weill and the Stony Creek Summer Theatre; to the libraries at Harvard College, Yale University and the University of Chicago for access to their various theatre collections; and to all of Welles's above-mentioned collaborators, and the score of others, for making themselves available to be interviewed. I have used their exact language wherever possible and have quoted extensively from my interviews with them. They are the original sources and their language better expresses their thoughts than could any paraphrase of mine. But, above all, I am most grateful to Hortense and Roger Hill, who, from South Miami, Florida, gambled on the sincerity of a total stranger and put their entire collection of Wellesiana into my hands.

The Theatre
of
ORSON WELLES

1

Early Welles, 1931-36

Somebody strange has arrived from America; come and see what you think of it.

What, I asked, is it?

Tall, young, fat: says he's been with the Guild Theatre in New York. Don't believe a word of it, but he's interesting. I want him to give me an audition. Says he's been in Connemara with a donkey. . . .

We found, as he had hinted, a very tall young man with a chubby face, full powerful lips, and disconcerting Chinese eyes. His hands were enormous and beautifully shaped. . .The voice, with its brazen transatlantic sonority, was already that of a preacher, a leader, a man of power.[1]

The liar with the hint of a preacher—and man of power—was George Orson Welles, sixteen years of age, shouldering his way into the Dublin Gate Theatre with counterfeit credentials from the United States. A few years later he was to begin his professional career in America backed by even more counterfeit tales of triumph in Ireland, at the Gate and—no less—the Abbey. Hilton Edwards and Michael MacLiammoir, the managers of the Dublin Gate, giggled over Welles's transparent fib and let it pass; but the prevaricated saga of Welles's early years in the theatre, manufactured by himself and later enlarged by the ordinary process of mythmaking that surrounds men of genius, is still taken seriously and for granted. The plain truth about Welles's early years is, of course, flatter and colder than the legend, but still remarkable as testimonial to the gall, the drive, the genuine ability, and the extraordinary charisma that Welles commanded even as an adolescent.

For the managers of the Gate, Welles tried to pass as a Theater Guild star on vacation in Ireland who might be persuaded to amuse himself with a few guest appearances at their theater. This was in the summer of 1931. Later, when his account got a little more out of hand, he had it that he was asked — in fact begged — to appear, and that he was then persuaded to stay in Dublin for two years of acting and directing, playing leads at the Gate, staging plays for their Studio Theatre, and finally becoming the first foreigner ever to perform at the world-famous Abbey Theatre.

That is the Welles account. But from the letters he wrote to America during that Dublin visit, a check of the records of the Abbey and the Dublin Gate, and conversations with associates who remember, some corrections, and some background are in order.

Welles at School

The major source of information about Welles, before, during, and immediately after his Irish adventures, is Roger and Hortense Hill. Their concern for him had a long history. He was first brought to them as a student at the Todd School for Boys, Woodstock, Illinois, in 1926. Welles's father owned a hotel in nearby Grand Detour, and it was there that Annette Collins, a teacher at Todd, recruited Orson. The Hills were understandably leery of him because his older brother, Richard, had been dismissed from the school some ten years earlier for disciplinary reasons. Richard is also reputed to have been something of a prodigy in his own right, writing a life of Christ at an incredibly young age; but like Orson's paper on "The Universal History of the Drama" (at age 8) and his critical study of Zarathustra (at age 10), this is another of those stories that cannot be corroborated. Both boys were born in Kenosha, Wisconsin, Orson on May 6, 1915.

Despite his brother's reputation, the Hills were much too impressed with Orson to block his admission to Todd. Hortense Hill recalls their first meeting:

> When I first saw him at ten years old he was dressed as Sherlock Holmes. He came into our living room and was introduced. I thought he was a cute little round-faced boy. As I got to know him more and found out out demanding he was, I learned how much of a problem it was going to be just keeping him a little bit under.

The Todd School for Boys was founded by Richard Kimble Todd in 1848, and he guided its progress for over half a century. Later, it was sold to Noble Hill, Roger's father. The school, which ended with the tenth grade, nevertheless provided its graduates with sufficient credentials to enter college. Roger was persuaded "to give up the advertising racket and try out pedagogy, for which I was ill-prepared. I said I would take over an English class, but mainly I wanted to work in extracurricular activities — drama and sports." He had his own theories about dramatic training:

A smiling Orson, hand on his chin, shortly after his admission to Todd in 1926. Annette Collins, who recruited him, is in the second row, far right. *Courtesy of Hortense and Roger Hill.*

I felt that the ordinary audience for school shows was worse than none at all because it consisted of parents and friends who were completely uncritical. So, we organized the Todd Troupers and started taking shows out of town. We would rent the Goodman Theatre in Chicago or use some of the suburban movie houses in the area.

In addition to these traveling productions we put on weekly shows in our own theater. These were unheralded and unsung. Our audiences were students, parents, friends.

Welles participated avidly in the Todd Troupers, and "by the time he was a senior was virtually directing them. And, of course, he was a star with the company from the time he was thirteen."

Even so, the majority of Welles's work was done in the "unofficial" weekly productions, where, for three years, he was in complete and undisputed control. It was here that he presented Molière's *The Physician in Spite of Himself,* his first version of *Dr. Faustus,* and "a very modern and mystical production of *Everyman,*" the scenery for which was an arrangement of platforms and stepladders. The habit of surrounding himself with disciples ("slaves," as John Houseman prefers to think of them) also seems to have begun about this time. Probably the first of these was Edgerton Paul, who later appeared with Welles in *Hearts of Age* and many of the W.P.A. and Mercury productions.

Shortly before his fifteenth birthday, Welles marked up a borrowed copy of *The Complete Works of William Shakespeare.* His most immediate concern was simply to provide the Todd Troupers with another of their widely acclaimed condensations of Shakespeare. The vehicle being readied in this instance, however, was *Winter of Discontent,* Welles's schoolboy antecedent of *Five Kings.*

Beginning with act 4, scene 7 of *3 Henry VI,* he reduced that play and *Richard III* to where they could both be performed within forty-five minutes. (Actually, this was more Part Two of *Five Kings,* which was never again produced, than Part One, which was.) Welles himself resolved to play Richard Plantagenet. He was already displaying a particular fascination for characters with a highly developed sense of evil.

There are several rather obvious advantages in performing *3 Henry VI* and *Richard III* together. Foremost among them is that so many of the background events that one needs to know in *Richard III* are dealt with in the earlier play: Clarence's defection, the murders of Henry and his son, the unfortunate circumstances of Edward's marriage. But in Welles's version none of these mattered. He discarded dramatic patterns and moral histories alike, opting instead for what A. P. Rossiter was later to refer to as "quasi-realistic, costume-play stuff."[2]

The sheer delight in Richard's villainy was at the heart of his editing, and he used the Shakespeare texts primarily as a bridge for

Welles as a not-so-lean-and-hungry Cassius exhorting a fellow schoolboy Brutus in the 1928 Todd Troupers production of *Julius Caesar. Courtesy of Hortense and Roger Hill.*

Welles as Richard Plantaganet in his own 1930 schoolboy production of *Winter of Discontent. Courtesy of Hortense and Roger Hill.*

linking one heinous crime to another. Without the stultifying elaboratness that was to plague his Mercury-Theatre Guild production of *Five Kings*, Welles was in all his schoolboy glory where, as Richard (in grotesque makeup), he could be

> the demon-Prince, the cacodemon born of Hell, the misshapen toad, etc. (all things ugly and ill). But through his prowess as an actor and his embodiment of the comic Vice and impish-to-fiendish humour, he offers the false as more attractive than the true (the actor's function), and the ugly and evil as admirable and amusing (the clown's game of value-reversals).[3]

Todd provided Welles with many valuable experiences. He was able to explore and experiment in an atmosphere of acceptance and encouragement. In addition to a theater the school's own radio station was at his disposal. "He pretty much educated himself," Hill admits. "I don't take any credit for Welles at all." There are few boarding schools that he would not have been miserable in; Todd luckily happened to be one of them.

> Take, for instance, the year he came to us. There was no swimming pool at Todd. Later, we built quite an elaborate one. He told us the next year it was the most crucifying thing that had ever happened to him. He'd told everybody that the reason he hadn't gone out for football or anything was because he was a great swimmer. Now, he had to build up the story that he was a mountain climber instead.

Welles was graduated from Todd in June 1931; he was sixteen years old. Hill and his official guardian, Dr. Maurice Bernstein, were faced with the dilemma of what to do with him next, and they agreed that he should continue his education. Welles's bent from earliest childhood had been toward the theatre, and this was confirmed at Todd. So Hill arranged for him to attend George Pierce Baker's famous Drama 47 Workshop. Bernstein, however, took exception to this arrangement, and for some undocumented reason decided upon Cornell University instead. The doctor, it should be noted, besides having a strong hold on young Orson's affections (although not so strong as that of the Hills), was also the executor of his father's estate. It was this control of the purse strings that finally decided Welles's movements immediately following his graduation and resulted in his going off to Ireland.

Welles left for Ireland in August of 1931, ostensibly on a painting trip, and stayed a scant six months. He did act at the Dublin Gate Theatre, but contrary to his account, never appeared at the Abbey for the substantial reason that the company was out of the country then, and touring in America. Nor did he direct any productions at the Gate's Studio Theatre (as Peter Cowie states in *The Cinema of Orson Welles* and Joseph McBride repeats in his book) for the equally good reason that there was none.

Welles in Ireland

But the decisive bit of chicanery that Welles perpetrated in the summer of 1931 was not on the management of the Dublin Gate Theatre but upon his guardian in Ravinia, Illinois.

In a letter to Roger Hill written aboard the White Star Line's S.S. *Baltic* on the eve of his arrival in Galway Bay ("a tiny out-post of the wild-west coast—Connemara, in County Mayo"), Welles described his departure from the Bernstein household:

It all happened so suddenly — three days of particularly vicious domestic war-fare — during which time I tried vainly to get in touch with you, ended in a roundtable conference which found all the principal powers as determined as ever. Dadda [his nickname for Bernstein] had thought the matter over and decided he could not permit my having ought to do with the diseased and dispicable theatre. [Everybody present] was uniformly and maddeningly derisive. Things went from bad to worse. Alternately I defended and offended. My head remained bloody but unbowed, and my nose, thanks to the thoughtful blooming of some neighboring clover (which I assured the enemy was ragweed!) began to sniffle hay-feverishly, and the household was illusioned into the realization that something had to be done.

It was then that Dadda arrived at a momentous decision — and in the spirit of true martyrdom chose the lesser of two great evils. Going abroad alone is not quite as unthinkable as joining the theatre — and so. . .I was whisked out of the fire into the frying pan. Four days later I was in New York!

A few months of walking and painting in Ireland and Scotland. . . and then on to England where there are schools — and theatres!!!!!!

His letters from Ireland are in a literary style vaguely reminiscent of the pre-Raphaelites.

Like Columbus, I, too, shall be followed by many. Civilization, like a gigantic spider, has thrown its web — or the beginnings of it — in the form of passable roads over the country-side and between mountains. [Letter to the Hills, September 1931]

Thoroughly enjoying his florid imagery, he continues the letter:

My, how verbose and bitter I grow!!!!! The latter is particularly inexcusable, for the Connacht, and all of the West as far as Sligo, has been revealed to me chaste and virgin — unsullied by a single hint of the impending sanitization and popularization, over which I have waxed so wordy.

Largely for the Hills' benefit (though one suspects that he delighted in surrendering himself to the pose), Welles created the character of a youthful aesthetic lost in the bliss of a pastoral setting, who is at the same time haunted by thoughts of an encroaching civilization. It was a part worthy of his acting talents, and he played it to the hilt.

With his luggage checked in Galway and assorted paints and brushes strapped to his back, Welles set out on foot for Clifden, the capital of Connemara. After only two miles of this, however, he wearily retraced his steps and purchased a donkey-cart on the excuse that it (and not walking) was the appropriate mode of transportation in these parts for an itinerant painter. His travels apparently brought him into contact with Issac O'Connaire, brother of Padriac Colum, and with "Mr. Cosgrove," president of the Irish Free State, whom he claims to have driven in his donkey-cart. (Cosgrove is even supposed to have carved a good-luck sun on the side of the cart to insure fair weather for his vagabond friend.)

That summer he visited the Aran Islands. During his stay there, Welles was forced to abandon, if only for the moment, what had become by now a characteristic pose. "Yesterday—for the first time, I checked up thoroughly on all my accounts—0." Undaunted, however, he immediately reverted to his literary posturings:

> The wind, the rain, the flies, to say nothing of the thousand and one diversions to which the adventurer in Ireland is tempted, were instrumental in the ruination and eventual physical demolishment of precisely ten terrible landscapes. [Letter to the Hills, September 4, 1931]

It is doubtful that he intended his letters to be taken seriously; they have about them an ingenuousness that is transparently a put-on. Still, he was in a very real sense reporting "home" and trying to justify his trip by establishing the fact that he was indeed painting. The letter continues:

> I am doing nothing but portraits now, and at the end of three weeks shall carry away with me perhaps a half dozen of them—simple sketches of men and women I have known here. Some of them will be bad pictures and some fair—most of them will be fair likenesses, but as portrayals of that undefinable Erin spirit they will all be dismal failures.

His last letter from the Aran Islands was addressed "My Dearest Dadda," and, like so many young runaways from home, he was "desperately in need of money. . .and unless financial aid awaits me in Dublin, I shall never be able to leave that city alive, but will die a swift but painful death by starvation. I have no ticket from New York to Chicago, remember, and Dublin is a long ways from the nearest seaport" (Letter to Bernstein, no date).

Because he was writing to people who were devoted to him, Welles was able to reveal an unashamed bravura and, at the same time, an obvious sense of dependency, even helplessness. He knew that his letters would be enjoyed and responded to sympathetically. But, above

all, he fully expected his needs to be met. This love of shared
pretense was to develop into artistic form in his work in the theatre
and, later, in film.

The Welles legend makes everything very simple: he arrived purpose-
fully in Dublin and met with instant success at the Gate Theatre.
Actually, he would have preferred to dally a while longer on his
painting tour, and expressed his regrets at not being able to in an
undated letter from the Aran Islands to Hortense Hill:

> Life has attained a symplicity and is lived with an artistry surpassing
> anything, I am sure, in the South Seas. There may be spots on
> globe where existence is as beautiful, but only where, contrary to the
> case here in Aran, it is easiest. Somewhere, too, there may be a
> forgotten land where eyes are as clear and hearts as open, but
> nowhere so remarkably combined with intelligence.

> You may gather that my wanderings have brought me to a kind of
> lost Eden rich in romance and bounteous beauty—and so indeed they
> have.

> I know and love every spot and every soul on these islands—so
> well, indeed, that when the steamer comes by again, as all too soon
> it must, I shall find it very hard to leave my little cottage by the
> sea. . . .

> When my pocket-book drags me back to the mainland, as it will
> this week's end, I will find myself with not half-a-dozen sketches to
> show for what was to have been a month's *work*. The more inspiring
> my surroundings the less and worse I paint!

He arrived in Dublin broke and with his morale at a low ebb.
His diary, begun on September 9th with a rapturous description of a barge
trip down the Shannon River, then told only of loneliness and despair:

> I am grateful that the electricity was off when I came back to
> my room that first evening in Dublin two days ago. If there had been
> light I would have sat down to this desk then and poured out the
> anguish that was in my soul—the anguish one experiences when
> unknown and alone in a big city and apparently forgotten at home.

Like the letters, his diary was a report back home. He was always
conscious of his readers, and his self-pity was a calculated bid for their
sympathies. There is a detailed description of his visit to the American
Express Office where no mail awaited him. Obviously feeling abused by
this oversight, he wanted Dadda and the Hills to be properly ashamed
of themselves. A later entry in his diary (undated, probably late

September 1931) suggests that he had developed a stoicism in the face
of utter despair:

A great deal happens here which will never go on record.

Indeed, it is just as well — not that the loneliness, boredom, terror
and hopes that the *very big* city of Dublin has caused me haven't
been intense at times, and even varied, but as I survey these past
(nearly!) three weeks I feel that the amount of things accomplished
or pleasure gained so little that an account of my squanderings of
time and money would only prove depressing reading in the years to
come.

In a nut shell what has happened is this: I have landed a job in
the Gate Theatre and plan to work there and go to Trinity [College]
until Christmas at least. But "landing" the job has been no speedy
process. I shall not go into it.

Suffice to say I have landed the job and tomorrow is casting. I have
been promised Karl Alexander, the second largest role (in *Jew Suss*).
And thereon hangs a tale!

This is, of course, a rather charming and fanciful bit of self-
dramatization. Having committed himself to the pose of an unhappy and
dejected young man, Welles lost interest in the diary as soon as he began
his activities at the Gate Theatre. But writing for a possible posterity, he
felt obliged to apologize for the fact that he had petered out early in
what was to have been a complete account of his stay in Ireland.

Unconstrained by the literary excesses in his diary, Welles later wrote
to Roger Hill a twenty-eight-page illustrated summary of the events
leading up to and including his involvement with the Gate Theatre. It
is apparently similar to one written to Dr. Bernstein (now lost or unavail-
able); however, the letter to Hill has a charm and a boyish candor that
the "official" report is said to have been devoid of.

A donkey-cart, a bicycle, a porter barge and a gypsy caravan have
taken me round and round Ireland and finally dumped me — as Dadda
must by this time have told you — in the Gate Theatre, Dublin.
Here I shall probably remain until Christmas and, more probably,
Spring — playing, painting scenery and signs, and writing publicity for
the press. [Undated, probably early October 1931]

Far from being the conquering hero of legend, Welles was, in fact,
employed much as any apprentice would be during his first season at
summer stock. (The Mercury Theatre of later years must have begun with

the same sense of excitement for others that Welles found at the Dublin Gate.) Despite his guardian's best efforts, Welles was now working in the theatre and conscious of the need to prove the legitimacy of his experience.

Here is the opportunity I have been praying for. The Gate is just organized [*sic*]. We are a kind of Irish Theatre Guild — that is to say, an art theatre on a commercial basis. Mr. Hilton Edwards and the equally famous Michael MacLiammoir head a producing staff and acting company of really excellent professionals. . .they represent the best of that vast army whom the talkies have reduced to job-hunting.

About the time I came along, Lord Longford, Lord Glenavy, Norman Reddin and many other Irish muckymucks had decided that the Gate was worth more than a summer's showing. They had the amusement tax lifted and they chipped in a *bit* of endowment, and Edwards and Company discovered that what had been originally a holiday spree was now a paying business. Most of the people have lingered and more have come — willing to put up with tiny salaries for the privilege of playing in worthwhile things. . . .I really didn't think such a company existed, where people were serious-minded and well-educated and highly-intelligent, and combined those virtues with the more cardinal sense of humour. It sounds Utopian, and it is.

Everybody works for the joy of working, the phrase "nobody works for the money" being *particularly applicable*. Salaries are of chorus girls' dimensions and all the same amount regardless of one's position. [Letter to Hill, undated, probably early October 1931]

It would have been unnecessary for Welles to try to convince Edwards and MacLiammoir that he was a star with the Theatre Guild. A theatre such as the Gate is always in need of willing and able workers, and, to a very real extent, they took full advantage of his youthful enthusiasm.

Welles was introduced to Hilton Edwards by Cathral O'Callaigh, whom he had known in the North. O'Callaigh was now playing small roles at the Gate Theatre.

There was much talk and finally an application for a job. He [Edwards] was gracious and candid. He would be delighted, he said, but the budget would not permit another member. He could find me a small part in *Jew Süss*, just going into rehearsal, but I would have to work on amateurs' wages — which are just a gesture. If I cared to stick and if we got along to-gether, bigger roles might come and he might even persuade the committee to pay me an extra Guinea. I accepted. [Letter to Hill, undated, probably early October 1931]

Luckily for Welles, Edwards was pretty much at a loss over the casting of Karl Alexander in *Jew Süss*. Welles had eyed the role wistfully and in time was asked to audition for it. Michael MacLiammoir remembers his audition as "an astonishing performance, wrong from beginning to end, but with all the qualities of fine acting, tearing their way through a chaos of inexperience."[4]

Welles's own description of that audition was far less laudatory:

I read them a scene. And being as I was terribly nervous and anxious to impress them, I performed a kind of J. Worthington Ham Karl Alexander with all the tricks and all the golden resonance I could conjure up.

Edwards did not immediately sieze on Welles's acting talents; in fact, he was not selected for the part until circumstance made him the only available choice. In addition, Edwards is supposed to have given him the part on the proviso that Welles promise not to "obey me blindly, but listen to me. More important still, listen to yourself. I can help you play the part, but you must see and hear what's good about yourself and what's lousy." Welles's reply: "But I know that already."

The effect upon Welles of being cast in the part is reflected in these passages from his October 1931 letter to the Hills.

The real climax to this whole thing is that Charles Marford — actor, press-agent and assistant scene-painter — has left and I am hired in his place to fill the various departments in which he functioned! Step back John Barrymore, Gordon Craig and John Clayton. Your day has passed. A new glory glows in the East!!! *I AM A PROFESSIONAL!!!*

Far from being self-assured at rehearsals, Welles was primarily anxious to please in order to maintain his status with the company:

I have done some more work on *Jew Süss* and it, thank God, is satisfactory! I followed directions implicitly — much against my will. (I can see already that my artistic-?-conscience is going to lead me into some disasterous and drastic differences of opinion.)

One gets the distinct impression that Welles expected to be rewarded in accordance with the degree of congeniality that he showed toward the Gate management, rather than as the result of his success in the role.

Judging by his reviews, he turned in a highly creditable performance. (It should be noted, however, that in reading over the reviews of the six productions he appeared in at the Gate Theatre between October 1931 and February 1932, one finds scarcely a harsh word about any of

His sketch of himself as the Duke in *Jew Süss. Courtesy of Orson Welles.*

them or their casts. The zeal of the Dublin press was more patriotic than critical, at least for the Gate.) Welles's most exorbitant praise came from the *Irish Independent*:

> His was a notable performance. There are few more unpleasant characters in dramatic literature than Karl Alexander, Duke of Wurtemberg, but there was a touch of humanity and simplicity in his swinishness which in less expert hands might have been lost. It is this

quality that makes him tolerable. Orson Welles captured it magnificently, for he played the part with supreme naturalness.[5]

Only one critic preferred to withhold judgment of Welles's performance, saying only that "it will be necessary to see him in other parts before it can be said that he is the accomplished actor he seemed last night in a part that might have been made for him."[6]

Jew Süss was followed in November by David Sears's Gothic thriller *The Dead Ride Fast*. Welles appeared as Ralph Bentley, an American tourist who stumbles on a haunted House of Shame. This time the *Irish Independent* singled him out for qualified praise:

> Mr. Orson Welles is a great acquisition to the Gate, but he must not be given too many aged parts [he played the father of a grown daughter], as they keep him in a state of permanent self-intoxication. We all want to see Mr. Welles without a wig.[7]

After Karl Alexander, Welles was to play only "character" roles at the Gate—not because he was better suited for them (despite his extreme youth) but because Edwards and MacLiammoir were not about to be outshone on their own stage by other actors in leading roles.

He is mentioned in *The Archdupe* only as being among a huge cast that served its author well.

His role in *Mogu of the Desert* was also a minor one, but by this time he had established himself as a member of the company. The *Irish Times*, which had been watching his progress, found in Chosroes, the King of Persia, "another character which gives Mr. Orson Welles an excellent opportunity to use his fine physique and great voice to advantage."[8] And his steadfast admirer on the *Irish Independent* mentioned Chosroes as being one of the "two small parts faultlessly played."[9]

The Gate Theatre was strongly disposed toward exotic adventure stories and supernatural thrillers that season, and *Death Takes a Holiday* was very much in keeping with the general tone of their selections. So, too, was their practice of doing plays that showed off its management. Welles was relegated to a brief appearance as Baron Lamberto; even so, the *Irish Times* picked him out for "an excellent impersonation."[10]

Hamlet, with MacLiammoir in the title role, opened February 2, 1932, and ran for two weeks. Welles played the Ghost and Fortinbras; it was his last performance at the Gate before returning to America. Although "the Ghost has seldom been presented more movingly,"[11] it was hardly the role to attract much attention for him.

The critical encouragement that Welles received in *Jew Süss* was, in fact, rewarded with smaller and smaller roles and increasingly arduous production duties. Actress Betty Chancellor still believes that "Orson was not well treated at the Gate. He was so remarkably good, I think the management was jealous!" She also dismissed the stories about his appearing at the Abbey Theatre, but noted that "I think he did a short season at the Peacock Theatre, which is the Abbey's Studio Theatre."[12] In fact, in the Abbey's absence the Gate was operating the Peacock, and Edwards and MacLiammoir, obviously determined to get full value out of Welles, put him to work in its scene shop. He described his activities in a letter to Roger Hill:

> I am quite rushed these days [just before Christmas, 1931] as I am designing and superintending the construction and painting of scenery —all the scenery—in the Peacock, an art-theaterish stock company quite distinct from the Gate. As the bill is changed weekly, and my regular acting and publicity work for the Gate goes on all the same and all the time, I am kept in a perpetual state of sweaty bliss! [Undated letter]

While supposedly enjoying unparalled success as an actor, Welles wrote to Mrs. Hill of his homesickness for Todd:

> I am doing very well in the most important theatre of the Capitol City. I am playing at the moment the most gratifying role [Karl Alexander] in an extremely successful play. The press both in London and Dublin have been very kind to me, and the people likewise. To-night, for example, I took six curtain calls alone—with the gallery and pit shouting and stamping and calling out my name. . .My purpose in crowing so loudly is to make more forceful my assurance that if you could ever find a place for me at Todd, I'd take the next boat!!!! [Undated letter, probably October 1931]

His departure may have been precipitated by a fight with Edwards and MacLiammoir ("because they wouldn't let him play Othello"[13]); however, judging by the fact that they were later to join him in America for the summer season at Woodstock, Illinois, and still later, for the filming of *Othello* and the staging of *Chimes at Midnight*, Welles probably left the Gate on reasonably cordial terms with them. Indeed, however much the management may have used him, they all seem to have been genuinely fond of each other. Welles's "disconcerting Chinese eyes" had an obvious attraction for Edwards and MacLiammoir, and that, as much as anything, would have made it possible for them all to work together as long as they did.

A sixteen year old boy in the 1930's would have been unlikely to reveal such things to his family. To Mrs. Hill's concern about his private life, Welles replied from Ireland:

Sketch of himself at the Peacock Theatre functioning "in the capacity of ass't. ass't. scene-painter." *Courtesy of Orson Welles.*

The ending of your letter rather terrified me. I quote: "The only thing that might happen is that you might meet a brilliant person that was fascinating company that—". And there you end! No closing sentence—and, thank God, no stain of blood! What dire threat were you about to make and what sinister power stayed your hand?????

Seriously, my purse and honor are intact and will remain so as long as I confine myself to my present company. [Undated letter]

The underlying reason for his leaving the Gate Theatre is probably the result of his initial commitment to Dr. Bernstein:

My excuse for being here is that I am to attend Trinity. But Trinity has decided, I'm afraid, to let me down. There is still a chance of my worming into one of the others, but if, as well may be, I am disappointed, I shall have to map out a plan of education for myself, or else break my contract as early as possible and return to America and Cornell (University). [Letter to Hill, undated]

From Dublin, Welles went to England. Although his reviews had preceded him and London managers did indeed seem interested, a Ministry of Labour regulation denied him the necessary work permits. With no alternative, he set sail for America and there received a final crushing blow. No one in New York theatrical circles had so much as heard of his Irish exploits. So, tail between his legs, he returned to Chicago and the Hills.

Post-Ireland Interlude
The Hills were again faced with the troublesome problem of keeping him occupied. "To a certain extent I've always had the job of keeping this guy busy and out of my hair," said Roger Hill. The forthcoming Chicago Drama Festival Competition somewhat eased the predicament. Hill had already cut the text of *Twelfth Night* to the Festival's specifications, and he gave it to Welles to stage for the all-male Todd Troupers. (Hill added an introduction, which was later incorporated into the Mercury recording of the play.) Welles also designed the setting, which featured a twelve-foot-high storybook with pages that turned to provide the scene changes. (The idea for the set came from a production of Kenneth MacGowan's that Hill had seen some years before in Chicago.) *Twelfth Night* won first prize that year (1932). A short film excerpt from it is still in the Hills' possession. Unfortunately, Welles's original staging was not used, only his set. A small backdrop is completely covered with a bright stylized rendering of a London street. The style is vaguely post-Impressionistic, and above all one notices the

vivid patterns of unrealistic coloring (the story book is also stylized). Welles also narrated the film, and his voice sounds very much as it does today.

With the Festival now behind them, Hill had to find something else for Welles to do. He remembered being extremely impressed with Welles's reading of John Brown's farewell address, and since both men

Welles as Malvolio in his 1932 Todd Troupers production of *Twelfth Night. Courtesy of Hortense and Roger Hill.*

had some knowledge of the abolitionist movement, Hill suggested that they collaborate on a play about it. Hill wrote the first act, and Welles the rest. The play, *Marching Song*, is on the whole scattered and incoherent. It contains so much historical exposition as to take the form of a treatise on Civil War politics. Hill candidly admits that the play "is way too long. It's not a unified play at all. Might make a pretty damned good pageant, though."

The original storybook setting for *Twelfth Night. Courtesy of Hortense and Roger Hill.*

During the summer of 1932, the Hills set Welles up in an apartment in Chicago's Old Town District. In addition to *Twelfth Night*, Hill had also edited *Julius Caesar* and *The Merchant of Venice* for publication, as well as adding his own biography of Shakespeare, an introduction to the plays, an explanation of the quartos and folios, brief discussions of the plots, grammar, chronology — even a rebuttal to those who hold that Bacon wrote Shakespeare. Welles's contributions to this project, which became known as *Everybody's Shakespeare*, were its numerous lively-rough sketches and the essay "On Staging Shakespeare and on Shakespeare's Stage."

Base of a Venetian memorial pillar set against a clear sky. Entrances can be made from below by steps as though characters came up by gondola.

A sketch from *The Merchant of Venice* volume of *Everybody's Shakespeare. Courtesy of Hortense and Roger Hill.*

The plays were originally published by the Todd Press in 1934. Hill sold the copyright to Harpers, promising a fourth play (*Macbeth*) and others to be decided on later. In 1939 Harpers withdrew *Everybody's Shakespeare* and, capitalizing on Welles's recent notoriety, retitled the edition *The Mercury Shakespeare*. (The original by-line, which read "by Roger Hill and Orson Welles," was also reversed.) These four texts had a long and profitable life span, remaining in print until 1964.

Trouping with Katharine Cornell
In the fall of 1933, the Hills attended a party at the home of a Todd parent, Hazel Feldman Buchbinder. They took their young charge along, and before the evening was over he had struck up an acquaintance

with Thornton Wilder. Wilder recognized Welles as the "young American who had made such a success in Dublin"[14] and about whom his friend, Lord Longford of the Gate Theatre, had written. The two men went off drinking together and, by morning, Wilder provided Welles with three letters of introduction to various friends in New York — among them one to Alexander Woollcott, who, in turn, introduced him to Guthrie McClintic and Katherine Cornell. They were both much impressed with Welles and, after a long interview, invited him to join the tour they were planning for later that year.

The repertory was to consist of *Romeo and Juliet* and two Cornell standbys: *Candida* and *The Barretts of Wimpole Street*. Cornell's personal manager, Gertrude Macy, remembered:

> We had no difficulty in persuading Orson to play Marchbanks, but he was very reluctant to do the stuttering Barrett brother, Octavius. He would rather have done nothing than a minor part in that play.[15]

Roger Hill thought of Welles as hopelessly unsuitable for Marchbanks. "He could play *Jew Suss*, but not a normal sixteen year old boy." Macy disagrees:

> He was flamboyant, exciting and hammy. . .he gave an excellent performance. He should have been slight and delicate; yet, he was enormous and clumsy. However, he read his lines well, injected a true feeling into his performance and appealed to the general run of audiences who weren't tied to a preconceived concept of the role.

As Octavius, however, he did not fare nearly so well:

> He was just adequate, always reading his lines intelligently, but sloppy and careless as a member of that well-disciplined, strictly-ordered family. I personally believe that his sprained ankle on the day of our Los Angeles opening was contrived so that the audience would not have to see him in that very subordinate role.

Mercutio may have been more to Welles's liking. However, Macy wrote, "recalling the magnificence of Brian Aherne (who succeeded Orson in New York), one cannot say more about Orson. But he later made a very good Tybalt." (John Mason Brown of the *New York Post* disagreed. He noted that even Irving Morrow was "a much more satisfying Tybalt than was Orson Welles."[16])

The Cornell tour began in Buffalo, New York, on the 29th of November, 1933, and came to an end the following June 20th at the Brooklyn Opera House — after logging 16,853 miles and 225 performances from coast to coast. As for his conduct, Macy tells us:

I don't recall that he ever missed a performance, but he was often late and worried us. . . .He missed a train once in the Middle West, and he and John Hoyt took or chartered a flight to reach our next stand in time. This was terribly upsetting to Miss Cornell and the management who did not know until the last minute that these two actors would be there to perform. . . .After a performance in San Francisco one night, he [Welles] put on a wig, a moustache, a beard and flowing cape and paraded around the Mark Hopkins Hotel as some foreign dignitary. He was often up to such escapades.

During their layover in Indianapolis (March 29-31, 1934), Welles wrote a long and apologetic letter to Cornell, begging her forgiveness for his behavior. Although his act of contrition was for having missed a train in Chicago, he makes it clear that this was not the only issue:

I see that my boots are roughshod and that I've been galloping in them over peoples' sensibilities.

I see that I have been assertive and brutal and irreverant, and that the sins of deliberate commission are as nothing to these.

This of course is good for me, coming as I am, noisy and faltering, cut of the age of insolence — just as the discipline of this tour is good for me.

John Hoyt feels that Welles took to McClintic's direction only "reluctantly." "Orson at that time always played to the top row of the third balcony, both in make-up and projectivity. Guthrie was a very precious director vis-a-vis that sort of thing, and he directed everything for Kit [Cornell]'s sake. Guthrie never liked Orson, and he never liked Guthrie. And Guthrie never forgave him for some of his misbehaviors both before and on the tour."[17]

Welles may have won Hoyt over, but he was decidedly unpopular with the rest of the cast. Actress Brenda Forbes said of him:

He was gauche and tiresome. He was always talking about plans for his own theatre, or else wanting to "take over" any group he joined.[18]

It was in Cheyenne, Wyoming, that Welles learned that Cornell had decided not to go on to New York as originally planned, but to tour the South instead, dropping *Romeo and Juliet* in Cincinnati, and opening with it and *Candida* and another play (not *The Barretts*) in New York that autumn. He voiced his bitterness in a letter to Roger Hill: "That cooks my Manhattan opening that had been held out to me for this season."[19] (He still had no idea of his forthcoming demotion from Mercutio to Tybalt.)

The Woodstock Summer Theatre Festival

In this letter he began to formulate alternate plans. He would return to Woodstock and, together with Roger Hill, produce a summer of repertory.

> I have an idea. As a matter of fact it's an old idea of yours jazzed up some and improved and made practical, I think, by an addition. The addition is a regular. . .professional repertory company and the idea is, of course, the Summer Theatre School for Todd. . . .

> A splendid company of players, all very young—or at least, enthusiastic—could be brought to Woodstock quite easily, I think, to begin work on the First of July. They will be happy to work for their room and board and a few dollars a week. The extra incentive of the swimming pool, horses and a student group to produce plays with. . . should make the two summer months particularly desirable to them.

Welles already had the nucleus of his company in mind: Hilton Edwards and Michael MacLiammoir of the Dublin Gate Theatre. He wired them:

> Would you both join me for summer season at campus in Woodstock, Illinois? Three plays running for a fortnight each. *Hamlet* for Micheal, *Czar Paul* for Hilton, something for me so far undecided. I am trying my hand at production.[20]

Edwards and MacLiammoir were understandably reluctant to join the Woodstock venture at first. They were anxious to show their *Hamlet* to America; however, the circumstances were hardly ideal.

> "It won't be New York, he warned me", or Washington or Boston; it'll mean playing some little mid-Western town with Orson and a horde of stage struck students.

> "I think", I repeated; "it would be exciting to see America". "You've never wanted to go there before" Hilton said. "Only one thing could attract a person like you to America, the theatre, and you won't get that in a hick town. It'll be like the small towns in this country without the charm". . . . That night Hilton decided he wanted to go to America.[21]

> Despite their trepidations MacLiammoir records an enthusiastic reception for them in New York. "We were told we had sixteen appointments at various places at the same time, for lunch, for interviews, for radio talks, for rotary speeches, for Irish societies, for women's clubs. . . .And everywhere new friends were wanting you. 'When are you going to bring the Gate over; oh, soon, well why not now.' "

Welles also approached John Hoyt to join him, but Hoyt declined. "I wanted to go to Europe and felt the Woodstock thing was just harum-scarum."

Welles persuaded Roger Hill to underwrite the Festival. In an early letter to him, Welles outlined his idea for publicizing it:

Emphasize the mid-Victorian, mid-Western charm (now highly fashionable) of quaint old Woodstock (the oldest and the quaintest place within driving distance of Chicago, after all) and of the Opera house, which is a real museum piece. . .and turn Todd Town into a pilgrimage place, with Todd itself a part of the shrine, playing host to the guests with a hardy barbeque dinner before the theatre. What better and what more dignified way could you think of to show off Todd? [Letter dated February 12, 1934]

Wells wrote to Whitford Kane describing the plans for the Festival:

Roger Hill is putting up most of the money. He figures the idea is a good publicity stunt for his school. . .The plan will be largely supported by a School of the Drama having its headquarters on the Todd campus. . .The whole school would be useless and silly without somebody genuinely fine as the director. We very much want you for the job. . .Now of course we haven't a great deal of initial capital, and our offer may seem a little silly—but I think that by the time you figure say 6% of every tuition fee in the school (about $300.00) as well as all expenses it won't add up as miserably as it might. The actual salary is - and here I blush a little - $25.00 a week. . .The professional group won't be large. . .probably going to bring over Hilton and Michael from Dublin and some equally fine people from New York and in Chicago. [Letter dated March 14, 1934]

While enlarging on Welles's publicity plans, Hill obviously felt that they were more grandiose than practical as a means of justifying his investment. One suspects that this project was for him yet another way of humoring his star pupil.

I think I can go before the Woodstock Chamber of Commerce and enlist some support on the advanced sale of tickets. . . .Still, I repeat, $2,000 is my limit of gamble. You say you can raise $1,000. With no expenses for housing or theatre (although it will take a few hundred dollars to remodel the Opera house dressing rooms and stage rigging) we should be able to swing it. But season contracts should, I'm sure, be avoided at this stage. [Letter, Hill to Welles, undated]

Hill undoubtedly would have been grateful for a way out when he received a letter from Welles informing him that Kane had just left for

Hollywood. "Next morning I talked to Chub [Hiram Sherman] and found out that they're coming back the first of July. In ample time. There is a remote possible that Whit may stay on in pictures for a couple of months more, but he swears there isn't much chance of it" (Letter dated May 1934). Hill's anxieties worsened when neither Kane nor Sherman appeared in Woodstock that summer.

Despite the fact that many of Welles's initial plans fell through, the season was surprisingly successful—meaning that it paid for itself and Roger Hill did not go broke.

> This in the depth of the Depression and bucking the great Chicago Century of Progress. Our luck was largely because of one man: John Clayton. "Forget the drama critics" he told me. (I was counting on my friendship with Ashton Stevens and other Chicago luminaries to put us over.) "Your only hope of not going broke is to dominate the society columns throughout the summer. Can you afford five hundred bucks for a big initial party? If so, I think I can put it over." Go ahead I said, I'm in so deep now I can't back out. "Fine. Waiter bring us a sheet of paper". This supplied, he went on: "Here is your list of sponsors." Then he wrote down every prominent society name in Chicago and Lake Forest. He brushed off my countryboy query with "they love it. They'll sponsor anything that costs them nothing and cracks the papers. . . .
>
> So we had a nice party. But to the uninitiated, nothing spectacular. I drove home feeling that another five hundred had slipped down the drain. Then came the Sunday papers: "Last Friday night the Tavern Club beheld the gayest, smartest, the wittiest assemblage of ambrosia imbibers since the last gathering on Mount Olympus." From then on throughout the summer sleepy picturesque Woodstock, sixty miles out in the sticks, became the favorite subject of news starved society editors. Marshall Fields ran full-page ads on what to wear at the openings. We were made.[22]

Woodstock became "the in-thing to do" that Welles had dreamed of. Both local papers and the Chicago press rushed to the Festival support. The *Woodstock Journal* pointed with pride to the fact that "many Woodstock folk who have demonstrated their interest in literature and other intellectual pursuits were present rubbing elbows with the out of town intelligencia."[23] The Chicago press found Woodstock a quaint experience. "Chicago was getting its first taste of summer barnstorming, and Chicago, a bit bedraggled and definitely wilting more with each act, liked the experience so much that it will probably repeat the whole gallant gesture."[24] While Woodstock looked up to the greater sophistication of its big-city neighbor, Chicago in turn compared itself with New York:

If Chicago supports the Todd Theatre Festival opening tonight as enthusiastically as New Yorkers support the several country theatre companies that spring up each summer within motoring distance of New York, tonight's pilgrimage to the old town of Woodstock will be the first of many similar ones that socialites will make during the next six weeks.[25]

Woodstock and Chicago society columns were full that summer of accounts of dinners given before the theatre for various social notables by various social notables. The Woodstock papers preferred to enthuse over the wonder of it all rather than actually reviewing the productions. The Chicago papers also went out of their way to be kind (if condescending), and one suspects that they were kinder to the productions (with their largely amateur casts) than was warranted. Claudia Cassidy of the *Chicago Journal of Commerce* seems to have spent the entire season in a state of shock over the mere fact of traveling so far from her city haunts. Of *Trilby*, she said that it "fit amusingly into the building whose vintage is no more disguised by its red and white paint than an old wine is changed by washing the dusty bottle."

Lloyd Lewis of the *Chicago Daily News* was more restrained. "Mr. Welles shows remarkable vigor of imagination and dramatic instinct, and with regimentation of his industry he will, I think, go far on the stage." Lewis looked on the Todd enterprise both with favor "as a pleasant motor objective" and with anticipation that "the citizens will in time find the town's dramatic prominence as interesting as did the reputedly 'great folk' who came from the big, wicked city."[26]

Hamlet continued to draw the crowds that *Trilby* had. The *Woodstock Journal* was duly impressed by both "Mr. Edwards, distinguished actor, director, and musician whose art and whose sincerity have brought him fame over-seas," and Mr. MacLiammoir, "whom substantial critics considered the best living player of Hamlet." The Journal was also pleased to learn from Edwards that "they will endeavor. . .to give the same performance given in Dublin."[27]

Publicity for the productions began to appear side-by-side with the world news. On August 2 a *Woodstock Sentinel* publicity item about *Hamlet* appeared alongside a picture of "DILLINGER'S NEMESIS," the chief of the Chicago office of the Department of Justice. (John Dillinger, after having been traced to the Chicago area had just been gunned down by federal agents.)

The announcement of *Tsar Paul* was featured with quite another kind of news item: "MacLiammoir Is Godfather to Baby."

The August 16 edition of the *Woodstock Journal* reported that "Orson Welles will leave for a vacation in Wisconsin. Hilton Edwards and Michael MacLiammoir will embark on the Santa Fe to see America."

As Svengali in his Woodstock Summer Theatre production of *Trilby. Courtesy of Hortense and Roger Hill.*

The *Journal* article went on to mention that "students of the summer school of the Todd Theatre will present another play—*The Drunkard*, directed by Charles O'Neil." Peter Cowie attributes *The Drunkard* to Welles. In fact, Welles had almost nothing to do with this production, making only a "cameo appearance" as one of a group of drinkers in the very last performance.

The Festival productions were by no means elaborate, but, as Hill described them:

> We did a pretty good job. The shows were practically all built and painted by students, although we had a few carpenters. . . .He [MacLiammoir, who designed the sets for *Hamlet* and *Tsar Paul*] said we had a much better stage than he and Edwards were used to. What we were doing was copying their productions. They'd give us the sketches of what they had done at the Gate, and we more or less went by that.[28]

Michael MacLiammoir (as Hamlet), Lois Prussing (as Gertrude), and Welles (as Claudius) in the Woodstock Summer Theatre production of *Hamlet. Courtesy of Hortense and Roger Hill.*

Welles's First Film

Throughout the summer Woodstock society columns detailed the participation of the Nicholson family in the festivities.

> On Saturday night Miss Virginia Nicholson, debutante daughter of Mr. and Mrs. Leo Nicholson of Wheaton, who has been attending the Todd Theatre School and acting as understudy for Miss Constance Heron was given the opportunity to play the part of Elizabeth in *Tsar Paul*. Miss Nicholson played that part with a great deal of fire and warmth and proved to be an actress of great potential ability. Sunday night, her father, Leo Nicholson, and a party from Wheaton drove over to see their daughter's first appearance with the professional theatre.[29]

Quite unawares, Virginia Nicholson became a part of motion picture history that August as a result of her appearance in *Hearts of Age*, Welles's first film, a silent, black and white one-reeler. It is a pastiche of images (candelabra, tolling bells, tombstones, clawing hands, and so forth). The sequences are assembled with little apparent thought toward creating a coherent narrative. Virginia and her husband-to-be (both heavily made up to simulate extreme age) tromp about the Todd campus. She takes up a perch atop a huge bell, while he careens time and again down a flight of fire-escape steps. The film ends in a darkened living room with Virginia in a coffin and Welles banging away at a piano and mugging for the camera. (Actually, the last sequence is that of a pair of hands shifting through a pile of tombstone-shaped cards until one bearing the legend "The End" is turned up.) *Hearts of Age* has some interesting features, such as contrasting real images with live drawings (by Welles); however, it is hard to say exactly how much of a directorial hand Welles actually had in its making.

Virginia Nicholson had earlier captivated Welles by choosing for her audition to the Woodstock Theatre Festival a speech from *1 Henry IV*. Before the summer was over she would become the first Mrs. Orson Welles. Now Virginia Pringle, she writes:

> It [*Hearts of Age*] was all a joke. There was no script. Orson simply amused himself thinking up totally unrelated sequences to be shot a la grand guignol. Bill Vance, who owned both film and camera, was a movie fiend in those days and went around shooting reel after reel of happenings mainly invented by Orson over a drink.[30]

Despite the fact that the end result may have been largely unplanned and the scarcity of information regarding who did what (the editing, for instance), *Hearts of Age* remains strangely provocative. Granted, it is a disconnected assemblage of primitive technique and trite imagery; never-

Welles in *Hearts of Age. Courtesy of Hortense and Roger Hill.*

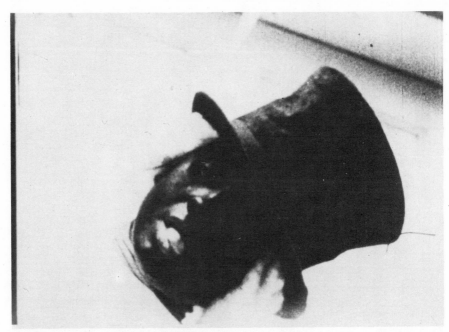

Edgerton Paul's suicide. . .

. . .and Welles's sketch of it in *Hearts of Age. Courtesy of Hortense and Roger Hill.*

theless, film historians at both the Greenwich Public Library (who received it as part of a bequest from Vance's estate) and the American Film Institute in Washington are currently examining it. Virginia Welles Pringle notwithstanding, the film has the same Gothic thriller atmosphere that was to pervade much of Welles later work.[31]

They rejoined the Cornell tour in Detroit that fall, only to learn that Brian Aherne had replaced Welles as Mercutio and that he had been demoted to the role of Tybalt.

Orson thought Brian Aherne was a terrible actor and very much resented losing Mercutio to him. He made Tybalt outstanding, however, and the changes of roles didn't hurt him at all. Aherne was absolutely necessary to Kit Cornell as Robert Browning in *The Barretts of Wimpole Street* and being something of a star, he wouldn't join the company unless he played Mercutio.[32]

Among those who attended his performance in New York as Tybalt was John Houseman, the Roumanian-born producer, whose recent staging of the Gertrude Stein-Virgil Thomson opera *Four Saints in Three Acts* had earned him a certain reputation among the American avant-garde. Houseman was casting around for an actor to portray the role of MacGafferty in Archibald MacLeish's *Panic*. The play (with Welles in it) lasted only three performances. But, far more importantly, it served to bring Houseman and Welles into the collaboration that was to result in such celebrated productions as the "Voodoo" *Macbeth* and *The Cradle Will Rock* for the W.P.A., *Julius Caesar* and *Five Kings* for their own Mercury Theatre, the *"War of the Worlds"* broadcast, and *Citizen Kane*.

2

The "Voodoo" *Macbeth*

In his recent book of memoirs, John Houseman, director of the W.P.A.'s Negro Theatre Project, described its splitting into two groups, one of which was to devote itself to "the performance of classical works of which our actors would be the interpretors, without concession or reference to color." For this fine scheme to work, there had to be one essential condition—that the quality of the productions be outstanding. To fulfill this last requirement a director in whose creative imagination Houseman had complete confidence was needed. He invited Orson Welles to join him on the Project. Houseman and Welles had entertained long-standing, if somewhat nebulous, plans for the staging of Elizabethan dramas. Welles accepted immediately, and, at the little-used Lafayette Theatre in Harlem, they began a partnership under some of the most peculiar but attractive conditions—"with Uncle Sam as our angel."[1]

All the Mercury offerings bore the credit line, "Production by Orson Welles," implying that he functioned not only as the director, but as designer, dramatist, and, most often, principle actor as well. To be sure, this generated a good bit of resentment among his collaborators (the designers, in particular). However in a more profound sense, that credit is, in fact, the only accurate description of a Welles production. The concepts that animated each of them originated with him and, moreover, were executed in such a way as to be subject to his absolute control.

Never a theoretician in his own right, Welles nonetheless personified Gordon Craig's dream of a master artist for the theatre. He reigned over his actors so that their talents served only his particular ends. In the few instances when such rigid control was impossible, he effectively reduced the importance of individual performance. Generally speaking, an actor's contribution to a play is to interpret the content of the script. In a Welles production, however, content served as little more than an obvious vehicle for its expressive form. Welles's real statement was contained in his violent imagery, and the actor became simply another facet of that imagery.

"The great directors all had great personal stories to tell," actor Norman Lloyd observed recently, "but not so with Welles."[2] Lloyd is recalling the time when most directors operated on the level of some private conceptual basis or other, and discounts Welles because of his reliance on the formal elements of the theatre. It is true that Welles was interested in the narrative content of his productions only insofar as they amplified his expressive concepts. However, his very handling of the theatre in so tactile a fashion — tactile in terms of a tumbling sensibility that was keyed to theatrical magic and hokum and so forth — resulted in profoundly personal statements that often could not be articulated rhetorically.

Welles was possessed of an imagination and sense of originality altogether unbounded by any theoretical restraints. Ideas came to him (and still do) catch-as-catch-can, with everything and anything being integrated into his production schemes. His theatrical vocabulary was at once the highest and the lowest and readily lent itself to those violent effects of contrast which were his signature. He was the sideshow barker wallowing in the high excitement and derring-do of the circus or variety theatre on the one hand, while simultaneously exercising austerity and disciplined understatement on the other.

In this, Welle's earliest production for the professional theatre, one can already discern a number of the qualities that would remain consistent throughout his career — foremost among them, his delight in sharing not only illusion but the mechanics of illusion with his audience.

Just as Welles was to take Herman Mankiewicz's script for *Citizen Kane* and turn it into a magic show, so, too, did he transform Shakespeare into a spectacle of thrills and sudden shocks. Audiences were drawn not so much to see the working out of Macbeth's tragic destiny as to experience the same undefined responses that make horror movies both ridiculous and yet still exhilarating. The impression it left in the theatre was that of a world steadily being consumed by the powers of darkness.

Whether in the theatre or in films, a Welles production always made creative use of sound. For example, in *Macbeth* the rhythmic pounding of jungle drums serves to accentuate the mounting tragedy. So, too, do the voodoo celebrants furnish a constant aural counterpoint to the events being visualized. The *primitive* violence of the drums is used to add dimension to the images of *civilized* violence onstage, or as ironic counterpoint when the action of the play falls into a momentary calm.

His use of sound both on the stage (*Macbeth*) and in the movies (*Citizen Kane*) is distinctly his own. He borrowed from radio the technique of introducing music into a scene as a kind of emotional prelude to the scene ahead. The transition from the coronation ball to the jungle realm of the witches is bridged in this way. While the waltz music is playing (and, incidently, establishing the play's period), the sound of the voodoo drums rises slowly, taking over only *after* the transition from one scene to the other has been completed.

This visual transition has been compared to a film dissolve and used to illustrate the influence of motion picture techniques on Welles's theatre. The fact is, of course, that the "influence" went the other way around. As early as *Macbeth*, he was already exploring on the stage techniques that were later to be heralded as original and innovative in his films.

It was Virginia Welles who first envisioned *Macbeth* as being set on the isle of Haiti in the early nineteenth century with voodoo priestesses as the witches, an inspiration that served as the jumping-off spot for her husband's version. Essentially, it provided the mechanism around which Welles embroidered his tale of black magic and frenzied voodoo celebrants.

The "Voodoo" *Macbeth* was conceived as a suspense thriller about a man who is manipulated by the forces of darkness. His nobility and conscience are overcome by the power of the witches, who control both Macbeth and the world he inhabits. And, unlike Shakespeare's play, there is none of the usual note of hope for a beleaguered country at the end.

His version of *Macbeth* was hardly tragic. Audiences were aroused by the production, but because he had stripped the text of its intellectual content, their response was wholly to the spectacle. *Macbeth* made its statement by evoking a world dominated by evil; the atmosphere of the production was transparently illusionistic, a nightmare more than a reality. From the outset of his work in the theatre, Welles played on his audience's current nightmare — the threat, to which it had become habituated — of fascism and impending war.

John Houseman has suggested that Welles found a striking parallel between Macbeth and the career of Henri Christophe, the Negro king of Haiti who killed himself when his cruelty led to a revolt. Welles was undoubtedly familiar with W. W. Harvey's *Sketches of Hayti*, written in 1827 and still regarded as the principle source of Welles's information on the life of Christophe. Harvey's most vivid memory of the island despot was the splendor in which he and his favorites lived:

All the officers in the army. . .were fond of dress to an extravagant degree, and often rendered their appearance ridiculous. Their coats were bedecked with gold and lace. . .their shoulders were burdened with epaulets of an enormous size; their caps were adorned with feathers nearly equalling their own weight: and these articles. . .rendered their appearance supremely fantastical.[3]

Nat Karson's sketch of the castle for the "Voodoo" *Macbeth. . .*

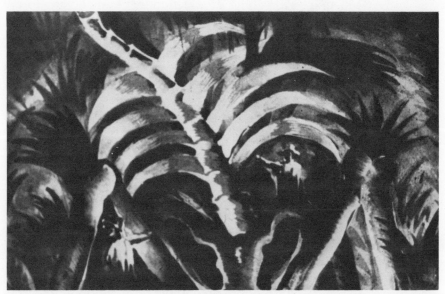

. . .and the jungle beyond. *Courtesy of the Federal Theatre Project Research Center, George Mason University, Fairfax, Virginia.*

Harvey could well have been describing Macbeth's court as it was to appear at the Lafayette Theatre over one hundred years later.

The jungle scenes are staged in front of a backdrop, behind which stands the permanent set — the castle. (There is a brief coastal scene, but it, too, is played before a drop.) By the use of light on the various levels of the set, Welles applied the movie technique of dissolves to the stage and, thus, created numerous scene changes.

Shakespeare's barren heath is replaced by a sinister tropical lushness. The play opens with Macbeth and Banquo thrashing their way through the leaves and tall grass. They are immediately confronted by Hecate (a male in Welles's text), the witches, and a circle of voodoo celebrants. After the prophesy, the scene fades to black on Hecate's "The charms wound up!" In that brief but highly charged moment, Macbeth's relationship with his fate is established, and all that follows is preordained.

The lights go up again, this time on the set itself. On the right is a tower connected to the palace by a bridge, which, in turn, becomes a gateway over the center entrance. Another ramp, this one over the battlements, leads to a door atop the tower (which is covered by a practical roof). The throne stands under the tower and faces the court-yard. In addition to these, there are several other entranceways, most notably a flight of stairs descending from the tower to the bridge and, then, on to the courtyard below.

Lady Macbeth is seen reading a letter from her husband amidst the distant sounds of thunder and lightning (an atmosphere that is to pervade the production). Macbeth and Banquo, along with Duncan and his entourage, come on, and straight off the murderous couple formulate their plan. Hardly any mention is made of Cawdor's revolt; Macbeth has been summarily elevated because the witches willed it so. This Lady Macbeth has none of the wifely sensibilities of her predecessor, but neither does she need them. Her very urgings are a part of the witches' charm and from the first she is obviously their tool. Shakespeare's entire scene was so edited by Welles as to leave only those features that were necessary for the working out of the curse. Because of the skill with which Welles handled them, his ideas, however far from Shakespeare's, seldom appear to be forced throughout the play.

Clearly, Macbeth's struggle with his conscience was of little interest to Welles, as the spell he is under precludes its being a real conflict. Like Faustus, he has, in effect, surrendered his soul, and in both instances the conflict between good and evil has been supplemented by a pattern of predetermination in which evil is entirely the governing force.

Visually this is depicted by positioning a band of cripples in Macbeth's open gateway. With their priest, they have come to receive the blessings of a holy king (the soon-to-be-assassinated Duncan, in Welles's text). Over their groans the witches' chant is heard, "All hail

Jack Carter and Edna Thomas as Macbeth and Lady Macbeth.
Courtesy of Edna Thomas.

Macbeth, King of Scotland." The priest closes the gates and locks himself out with the cripples, leaving the thane and his lady alone onstage surrounded by the faint pulsing of voodoo drums.

It is a vision of Hecate's dagger that Macbeth sees before him, while the witches' chanting coupled with the wail and throb of the voodoo celebrants create the dialogue that sends him off to the tower. Gusts of wind and flashes of lightning afterward punctuate his account of the crime. These evidences of the witches' power, as much as his own memory of the murder, haunt the guilty man.

In Welles's text the dead king has only one son, Malcolm, who, together with Macduff, flees to the coast. The scene of the discovery of Duncan's body is considerably shortened and is physically enlarged by the appearance onstage of his entire court. This includes Lady Macduff (no doubt because she will later be killed, not in her own castle but in Macbeth's). Welles takes further advantage of her presence by having her attempt to stay the two fugitives in their flight. Unsuccessful, she is left in tears upon their departure. Macbeth is seen walking the battlements as Macduff hurries Malcolm off, whereupon he comes down, crosses to the deserted throne, and slumps wretchedly into it.

The night's clamor gives way to the silence of early dawn. Against the melodramatic hullabaloo of the preceeding scene, Welles juxtaposed a single figure in the crack of light where the gate stands open. Then another figure appears and the two figures slowly, almost furtively, push the door open, dragging themselves into the courtyard. Another dozen or so follow suit. They are the cripples, this time without their priest. Macbeth watches in silent fascination as these piteous reminders of his own damnation falteringly make their way over to the throne and humble themselves before him.

While the cripples lie prostrate, the three witches stand huddled together on the castle wall like birds of prey and take up their hoarse chant to the steady throb of the drums. Hecate materializes atop the tower, silhouetted against the violent dawn that flames up behind him. Leaning over the throne below, he hurls his curse down upon Macbeth:

I will drain him dry as hay;
Sleep shall neither night nor day
Hang upon his penthouse lie;
   (Drums stop)
He shall live a man forbid!

One beat of a drum accents the very last syllable, and a blackout brings the first half of Welles's text to a close.

Part 2 opens with a flourish. The entire court—ladies, attendants, and all—is present at Macbeth's coronation. Welles had taken Shakespeare's banquet scene and converted it into a rousing ball with dance music. Virgil Thomson, the show's musical director, arranged an effective medley of Josef Lanner waltzes for this purpose. (Interestingly, most critics in writing about this scene insist that Welles used a recording of the "Blue Danube Waltz" for the musical background.)

Quickly, Welles progresses from the gala theatrical nuances of this scene to Banquo's open challenge. The omnipresent drums again swell momentarily, as Macbeth sits alone and brooding on his ill-gotten throne. The mocking chant, "Hail, King of Scotland!," is silenced by his panicked call to Seyton, who ushers in the two murderers. (In their all-enveloping black cloaks and tall stovepipe hats, they give the impression of having been summoned from the nether regions, rather than being agents of this world.) As they slip out to ambush Fleance and Banquo, Macbeth whispers jokingly into their ears, triggering a peal of laughter that echoes the witches' cacklings.

Until now, the witches' presence has been on a more or less symbolic level, with their appearance well distinguished from the otherwise realistic actions of the play. At this point, however, the supernatural takes on a human guise, as Hecate assumes the role of the third murderer. After the killing Hecate declares his intentions to rain "artificial spirits" down upon Macbeth, who "by the strength of their illusion/Shall draw him on in his confusion!"

As Hecate is uttering his curse, the first chords of a waltz rise faintly and weirdly; and as his light dim, others go up again on the ballroom. The music bursts forth, and the dancers pick up their blocking from the previous scene. The contrast is both striking and complete in every respect; in ambiance, in terms of space and sound, they are two entirely different worlds. Within the palace walls a layer of civilization, however treacherous, exists; while just outside, the jungle lies in waiting. Even the dancers, moving as they do in horizontal — that is to say, symmetrical — patterns, stand out against the more abandoned movements of their voodoo counterparts.

Elderly dignitaries arrive and are warmly greeted by the royal couple. It is only when they attempt to join in the dancing that Macbeth's fears overtake him. Banquo's ghost first appears from behind the tower, and grows in size to a huge mask filling the castle gate. Macbeth screams, causing the dancers to fall back on either side. He slumps to the foot of the throne as the court, murmuring sympathies, disperse. From afar, the drums steal in again. Suddenly Macbeth rises, determined "to know/By the worst means, the worse." An earsplitting clap of thunder follows, and the stage goes black. Whereupon the gateway swings open, framing Hecate in an eerie light. He beckons to Macbeth as the scene ends.

Hecate guides Macbeth through the grass and rank leaves to a clearing. Two half-circles of voodoo women obscure a smoking cauldron.

Jack Carter as Macbeth, and the two Murderers. *Courtesy of Edna Thomas.*

The three witches, raised slightly above stage level, are already in a state of ecstasy. The drums take up the chant, and the ritual, seen in strobe light, begins. The celebrants speak in the voices of their "controls," as the two half-circles became a full one moving around the cauldron. Possessed by the magic, Hecate conjures up seven apparitions for Macbeth, who stands transfixed before each one. With the first light of dawn, he is ordered to "give the edge o' the sword" to Lady Macduff and her children. Fearful again, Macbeth plunges back into the jungle, with Hecate pronouncing his final malediction upon him.

Whereas Shakespeare has Lady Macduff with only her son to face the murderers (again, two in number), Welles wrings the utmost pathos out of an already pathetic scene by adding to it a nurse and babe-in-arms. Mother and son are killed onstage, gunned down by giant blunder-blusses. The nurse, clutching the baby to her, runs off, with the murderers in pursuit. "Her cries echo through the palace. Then, there is an awful scream, and silence."[4]

Against a fence of grass blades, presumably the coast to which they have fled, Macduff assures Malcolm of his loyalty and learns of his family's slaughter.

The palace, now completely lorded over by the witches, is the setting for the remainder of the play. They attend Lady Macbeth as she walks in her sleep. It is Hecate, not Malcolm, who commands that every soldier hew him down a bough/And bear 't before him. . . ." For Welles, then, the battle that follows is not an uprising of oppressed peoples but, rather, the finale (using a few handy souls) to a series of events whose course had been determined from the very beginning.

Macbeth learns that Birnam Wood is, indeed, moving. And, almost as an afterthought, he is told of his wife's suicide. Slowly, palm trees rise over the battlements, with the jungle literally creeping through the open gate until the lower stage is filled by it. Macduff emerges from the foliage. The duel scene begins with pistols, and, when all shots have missed, turns to swords. There is a sudden silence broken, first, by the duel itself, and, after Macbeth had been run through, by the witches' cacklings. Macduff throws the severed head into the vegetation below. At this point the army puts down its branches and the "jungle" collapses, revealing a stage filled with people and Malcolm established on the throne.

Hecate and the witches catch Macbeth's head and raise it aloft gleefully. From offstage, the voodoo women pick up the chant, "All hail, Malcolm!" Unknowingly, the army joins in with a rousing chorus of "Hail, King of Scotland!" All—drums, army, voodoo celebrants—are instantly stilled as Hecate steps forward and once again declares, "The charms wound up!" In Malcolm the witches have found their latest victim, and on that dour note the play comes to an end.

Wardell Saunders as Malcolm (*right*) and Thomas Anderson as Ross (*left*) console Maurice Ellis as Macduff over the murders of Lady Macduff and their children. *Courtesy of the Federal Theatre Project Research Center, George Mason University, Fairfax, Virginia.*

Because *Macbeth* was produced under the auspices of the W.P.A., Welles was able to exploit many more resources than would have been available to him in a commercial venture. Percy Hammond in the *New York Herald-Tribune* (April 16, 1936) reported that Washington spared no expense to make *Macbeth* an ostentatious spectacle. In fact, the resources were not as limitless as he indicated. Fortunately, they were sufficient for Welles's purpose.

To the verdant tropical effects that so dominated the setting, designer Nat Karson dressed the hundred-member cast for a veritable fashion parade as well. Both the set and costumes were executed in W.P.A. workrooms at a cost of only two thousand dollars.

The witches holding up Macbeth's severed head. Malcolm is on the throne. A victorious Macduff stands atop the tower. *Courtesy of the Federal Theatre Project Research Center, George Mason · University, Fairfax, Virginia.*

An African witch doctor, known simply as Abdul, headed the troupe of voodoo drummers. Puppeteer Bil Baird still remembers him fondly as "an excitable little man who adorned himself in silver bracelets."[5] They got to know each other by speaking a kind of Creole French. Abdul and Asadata Dafora Horton, who supervised the voodoo chants and dances, had come to this country a few years before from Sierra Leone.

Chaos aside, the most hostile aspect of the production was a conflict of temperaments between Welles and his lighting designer, Abe Feder. According to Edna Thomas, "Orson was constantly on Feder's back, screaming away at him,"[6] and, indeed, Welles's own rehearsal notes corroborate this. "Light on steps typical Feder pink—terrible. . . . Light behind dancers too bright—light stinks. . . . Tell Feder light on Edna has terrible green value instead of white or lavender." It may be possible that Welles found these tactics appropriate for getting the effects he wanted. Certainly, hard feelings did not prevent the two men from working together again. (Feder, however, still looks back upon the experience with great bitterness.)

Individual performances, however minimized, were still beyond Welles's control. For one thing, the W.P.A.'s purpose was to give people work, and, as Edna Thomas described it, it seemed as though "anyone who could read lines was taken on." The *Macbeth* company included only four professional actors: Edna Thomas, Jack Carter, Eric Burroughs, and Canada Lee.

Mrs. Thomas's career had begun in the same Lafayette Theatre some fifteen years before with a Harlem stock company. Her other credits included touring in David Belasco's *Lulubelle*, as well as appearing with Helen Hayes in *Harriet*. For all her years in the theatre, however, this prominent Negro actress had never before attempted a major classical role. Lady Macbeth was "quite a step up" for her, but one she admits was never successfully taken.

The other three professionals had mixed backgrounds. Eric Burroughs, who was a graduate of the Royal Academy, played Hecate as a figure of evil assembled from fragments of witches' lines and equipped with a twelve-foot bullwhip. Jack Carter, who had received wide acclaim for his portrayal of Crown in the original *Porgy*, was Macbeth. Former lightweight boxing contender, Canada Lee, became the cigar-smoking Banquo.

The other members of the company were mainly community people, Harlemites who had drifted into the Negro Theatre Project. And everyone from Macbeth to the little boys who carried the swords on their shoulders received the same $23.86 per week.

Mrs. Thomas still refers to Welles as "a genius of a director," but believes that his angry scenes with Feder might have been repeated with the actors had *Macbeth* not been a W.P.A. project.

> For instance, he had me standing on the steps leading up to the castle, while he was rehearsing a group down on the stage—again and again and again doing what the situation called for. I don't remember what it was; I only remember the outcome of it. Orson began to get very abusive, until, finally, he said to me, "Darling, come down here. I'm not going to have you standing there all this time while these dumbbells aren't catching on." When I came down, I told him, "Orson, don't do that; those people will take your head off." And they would have.

Apparently, Welles realized it too, and took to handling "everybody with kid gloves."

Toward Mrs. Thomas and Jack Carter, in particular, Welles was always charming and considerate. Following rehearsals (sometimes ending after midnight), "he would like to take Jack and me out to the night

Eric Burroughs as Hecate. *Courtesy of the Federal Theatre Project Research Center, George Mason University, Fairfax, Virginia.*

spots, and sit in a corner and recite poetry." More often than not, that "poetry" was in the form of line readings from *Macbeth*. Mrs. Thomas expressed absolute confidence in Welles, and agreed with everything he did in his handling of her. This was not a universally shared opinion among his actors, as he was, after all, less interested in brilliant solo performances than in seeing that they did nothing to jar his production scheme.

Samuel Leve, who was later to design both *Julius Caesar* and *The Shoemaker's Holiday*, attended several rehearsals of *Macbeth* on Nat Karson's invitation and found them to be "absolute pandemonium, with Welles barking orders over the amplification system."[7] Hiram Sherman, one of Welles's earliest collaborators, was also in attendance and, while sharing Leve's impression, added wryly, "He [Welles] thrives on chaos, and still does to this very day."[8]

Welles's rehearsal notes were dictated to his wife, Virginia, who, afterward, would type them up. She explained her presence:

> Orson trusted my opinion and taste, and because if I didn't understand a thing, my reaction was fairly typical of the average audience.[9]

She remembers Welles as being "quite remarkable with actors. Lots of them have never given a decent performance since they left Orson's influence."

The notes themselves disclose particular attention to timing and blocking, as well as innumerable corrections of individual lines (primarily in an effort to impress proper emphasis upon bit of dialogue).

> Wardell [Saunders] down exactly on word, Malcolm. . . .Cut Eric's ministerial tone. . . .Edna should have a look over her shoulder as she crosses the ramp. . . ."To make up mind" not big enough.

Several pages of lighting cues illustrate his technical know-how.

> Fix number 15 hook-up to hit Macbeth in arch but not to spill. . .28—dim down and replug.

On the whole it is difficult to draw any conclusions from his notes. By themselves, they are not unlike those prepared by any hack company director. There are, however, glimpses of him urging his actors to "fix up" their performances.

Welles's chagrin is obvious when he, first, reminds Eric Burroughs to set his blocking and, then, asks coyly, "Is Hecate saving his voice?" Jack Carter may have been Welles's favorite, but that did not spare him from an occasional swipe: "Jesus Christ, Jack—learn your lines!. . . .TAKE

THE WEARINESS OUT OF YOUR BODY WHEN YOU GO UPSTAIRS
. . . .Jack railroading again."

Part of his production scheme involved the extensive use of music and sound effects calculated, in part, to build up the actors' voices.

Take bugle after Edna's cross. . . .What about the goddammed thunder?. . .What the hell happened to Virgil Thomson sound effects between the acts? Why wasn't it started sooner?. . .Thunder ending a little too high.

Virgil Thomson was one of the very few people not thrust on the production by the W.P.A. (The Negro Theatre orchestra was conducted by the noted black musician, Joe Jordan.) Thomson worked with Welles with equanimity:

He knew exactly the effect he wanted. He never told you how to produce it. You leave those things to people who have the technique.[10]

According to Thomson, the score consisted of Lanner waltzes (period music of the early 19th century) and "other hearts and flowers tunes." His own composition was limited to a number of fanfares. He is still quite unenthusiastic about the musical possibilities in Shakespeare, being convinced that Shakespeare "fixed" his plays so that no one could add much music beyond "a couple of trumpet calls for an off-stage battle and, maybe, one song." The opportunity for his "one song" (the waltzes) came about as the result of Welles's turning the banquet scene into a coronation.

In addition to the voodoo effects, there was a sizeable pit orchestra and, backstage, a group of percussion instruments made up in part of bass and kettle drums, a rain box, a thunder sheet, and a wind machine. This latter ensemble was not only for simulating storms, but also for accompanying some of the grander speeches.

Thomson, on the pretext of threatening weather, could support an actor's voice and even build it up to greater than life-size. He attributes this invention to Welles, but both were fully conscious of its problems. As a result of the percussion rattling, actors backstage were unable to hear lines and had to depend on the lights for cues. In addition, actors who were so accompanied could not change their readings much from night to night. On Thomson's insistence these percussion instruments were played by musicians and not stagehands, whose tendency is "to just bang away."

Thomson felt that the overall effect created by the storms, and the battle music, and the marching trees, and the voodoo celebrants was most melodramatic. Jean Cocteau, who saw the production in his company, found them to be simply distracting (especially the constant lighting changes) until he grasped their function as adding to the climate of violence.

The newspaper and magazine critics greeted the production with their own social and political biases rather than with artistic judgments. Errol Aubrey Jones, writing in the *New York Age,* a Harlem weekly, thought it was all marvelous, and cited a number of the actors for special honors. One suspects that he was rebuking critics of the Negro Theatre Project at least as much as he was heralding the production itself. Roi Otley of the *Amsterdam News* (April 18, 1936) left nothing to doubt. For him *Macbeth* "definitely justified its existence and made it clear that the government should continue to subsidize a Negro theatre project." He wrote condescendingly of the "presence of Broadway and Park Avenue in the theatre," adding:

> They could hardly be considered a particularly sympathetic audience for what was being revealed. . . .We therefore warn downtown visitors that the play is purely for Harlem consumption.

The one reservation he expressed was with the quality of some of the acting. Even so, the cast as a whole was never less than admirable in his opinion, while "the ensemble scenes were a joy to behold."

Much the same kind of enthusiasm was voiced by Willson Whitman in *Stage* (July 1936), who, in this and other reviews (*Class of '29, Murder in the Cathedral,* and *Triple a Plowed Under,* to name just a few), was trying her best to be as supportive of the W.P.A. as possible. But a ring of benevolent racism in her cheerful reception of *Macbeth,* transformed, as it was, to "the land of voodoo magic," is nonetheless apparent.

Edward R. Murrow's response in the same issue of *Stage,* attempted in effect, to out-liberal the liberal Miss Whitman. Murrow found in the production an insidious "blackface attitude," one that not only disregarded but burlesqued the "truer emotional roots" of the Negro people. He expressed the desire to see a Negro theatre that would show "the passion, beauty, cruelty, suffering, aspiration, frustration, humor, and, yes, victories of a deeply emotional race. . . ." But he did not judge *Macbeth* by any aesthetic standards.

Neither did Percy Hammond (*New York Herald Tribune,* April 16, 1936), but for quite different reasons. He criticized "the inability of so noble a race to sing the music of Shakespeare." While acknowledging Welles's reordering of the text to be both "startling and original," he dismissed the production only "as interesting as could be expected." Hammond's criticism may be a reflection of his objection to the idea that the federal government had spent so much money on one of "your benevolent Uncle Sam's experimental philanthropies."

Several reviewers liked the production well enough, but found the cast unequal to the task of performing Shakespeare. Burns Mantle and Arthur Polluck were among those who drew comparisons between *Macbeth* and *The Emperor Jones*. Richard Lockridge (*New York Sun*, April 15, 1936) expressed a certain pique at the idea of its being set in Haiti, remarking that "the cast acted in a manner in keeping with this challenging, if outlandish, exuberance of decor." On the other hand, for Robert Garland (*New York World Telegram*, April 15, 1936) "a lot of it [was] effervescent and all of it interesting." And, making no pretense at serious criticism, *Variety* (April 22, 1936) decided that "it is, in spite of everything, a good show."

Brooks Atkinson (*New York Times*, April 15, 1936) gave it a more thoughtful, if unfavorable, review, finding Welles's adaptation to be "more considerate of the text than such a free-hand occasion warrants." He was, however, refreshingly aware of Welles's intentions and, in general, believed the production to merit the excitement it was causing. The witches' scene, in particular, was singled out as "logical and stunning and a triumph of theatre art." Whatever their tone, Atkinson's remarks were directed toward artistic considerations.

John Mason Brown was much harsher. He thought that although the production was replete with possibilities, Welles did not carry them nearly far enough to suit him.

The pity is that this *Macbeth*, which should have been so interesting, wastes not only an exciting idea but murders an exciting play. [*New York Post*, April 15, 1936]

In a later column (April 18, 1936) he reiterated his feelings about the script, calling it "wretchedly cut and stupidly altered."

If the critics were generally negative to *Macbeth*, its audiences were not; in Harlem and on tour over 100,000 saw this production and reveled in it.

Macbeth was subjected to adverse criticism of a political nature as well. There can be no question that it was radical in the artistic sense, but this theatrical radicalism was extended by some into the social and political arena as well—a charge that is at best peripherally directed at Houseman and Welles.

That is not to say that their work was entirely without its political orientation; one of Welles's special gifts was bringing to theatrical life issues that most concerned his audiences. He and Houseman were working in the theatre at a time when it was possible to relate to current events, as has been true in all great theatrical eras.

While it is as inappropriate to classify Welles's theatre as political as it would be to do so with Shakespeare's, Houseman perhaps overstated the case when he declared, "Orson and I were totally unpolitical people. We ran two projects for the W.P.A. . . .and they were notorious for being non-political."

Despite Houseman's disclaimer, almost overnight, and, seemingly, with no predetermined idea of what it should be, he and Welles became the darlings of the radical movement. "We got into it by accident."

That "accident" began with *Macbeth*. Everything done in Harlem at the Negro Theatre Project was considered radical, simply because the situation was explosive and unique. Thus, a work of Shakespeare played by a black cast became a venture in radicalism. (Welles at this time also wanted to produce *Romeo and Juliet* for the Project, with one of the families to be black and the other white. This, unfortunately, never materialized.)

Comparison of Stage "Macbeth" and Film "Macbeth"

The "Voodoo" *Macbeth* was Welles's own perception of how he might best make use of Shakespeare. A comparison with the subsequent film version reveals that his basic understanding of the play remained much the same over the years.

Throughout his career Welles has turned again and again to the same materials. Often, as with *Five Kings* and *Julius Caesar*, his first exposure to them was as a pupil at the Todd School. *Macbeth* was no exception. But while he may have acted in it there (to say nothing of designing the scenery), the "Voodoo" *Macbeth* was his initial production of the play. It was not to be his last.

A number of the similarities between the film and stage versions can be accounted for by the fact that the texts of both were virtually the same, the only outstanding exception being the film's return to Shakespeare's Highland setting. As such, it was tried out at the Utah Centennial Festival in Salt Lake City prior to going before the cameras in 1948. Both versions were cut to approximately ninety minutes. The text for the Utah production had been planned along scenario lines, and carrying it over to film was just a short step. Thus, despite his own statements to the contrary, Welles found for this material—and later for *Five Kings*—a concept for one medium that was readily adaptable to the other.

Welles's fascination with *Macbeth* was a continuing one. In fact, his first directorial credit on radio was a half-hour abridgment of *Macbeth*, which he "arranged" for the CBS Columbia Workshop, February 28, 1937. He also appeared in the title role, with Edna Thomas as Lady Macbeth and Hiram Sherman as one of the three male witches. Not long afterward he repeated it, this time in *two* half-hour segments, using rhythmical sound effects rather than realistic sound. And three years after this he again turned to *Macbeth*, in a fuller recorded version, which included he and Roger Hill's *Mercury Shakespeare* edition of the script as a free bonus with the album.

Writing in *Sight and Sound*, Henry Raynor criticized the film for concentrating on Macbeth's devouring ambition and for presenting Macbeth as "a savage devoid of any moral scruples—a man not opposed to the idea of murder, just superstitiously afraid of it."[11] These remarks could as easily have been applied to the "voodoo" production.

Despite a spoken introduction to the film, which sets it in the early days of Scottish Christianity, the many similarities to the stage production are apparent. Macbeth himself is still a Faust-like character governed by harbingers of evil (two of them former Goldwyn Girls, and the third a man in drag); only here they lead him to murder, to the throne, and, finally, to his own decapitation through the manipulating of his figure in clay. The castle remains a place of evil design, filled with black shadows; and when the first Thane of Cawdor is beheaded, "half-naked men thunder like African natives on drums."[12]

Thus, in the dozen or so years that had elapsed between the stage and film versions of *Macbeth*, all that Welles seems to have done is vary his portrayal of the supernatural.

3

Horse Eats Hat

Many of John Houseman's theatrical acquaintances had banded together around him and Welles out of a vague, undefined feeling that they were helping to start something new and significant in the cultural life of the times. However, once the artistic challenge of a *Macbeth* had been met, the Negro Theatre Project clearly had little more to offer Welles. He began to dream of other worlds to conquer.

Thereupon, Houseman chose to abandon his position in order to "risk my whole future on a partnership with a twenty-year-old boy, in whose talent I had unquestioning faith, but with whom I must increasingly play the combined and tricky roles of producer, censor, advisor, impresario, father, older brother and bosom friend." He knew, also, that he had to provide new theatrical opportunities and "find fresh scope for Orson's terrible energy and boundless ambition, before someone else did."[1]

Houseman went to Hallie Flanagan, National Director of the Federal Theatre, with the proposal that he be allowed to start a classical Theatre Project, using the Maxine Elliott Theatre, which the W.P.A. had leased from the Shubert organization, as its base of operation. This became known as, simply, Project 891.

Initially, at least, Project 891 was a terrible disappointment to anyone expecting a political theatre. For his opening production Welles selected the century-old French farce *An Italian Straw Hat*, which he then proceeded to overhaul into a vehicle for a frankly libidinous slapstick spectacle. Knowing the particular kind of double entendre that would appeal to his audience, Welles integrated the immediacy of vaudeville into the play's farcical structure. The result was an imitation of a popular movie comedy re-created for the stage.

An Italian Straw Hat was chosen because Houseman and Welles wanted to establish a balanced repertory, but the production soon turned into Welles's personal joke.

74

Eugene Labiche enjoyed the reputation of being both the scourge and favorite playwright of the French bourgeoisie. His *Italian Straw Hat*, written in 1851 in collaboration with Marc-Michel, quickly became one one of nineteenth century's most durable entertainments. It was originally intended as a vaudeville about manners and morals that are recognizably mid-century French. Needless to say, a literal translation was not what Welles was looking for. Nor did the two free versions made by W. S. Gilbert, entitled, respectively, *The Wedding March* and *Haste to the Wedding*, stir his enthusiasm.

Virgil Thomson suggested that the adaptation be entrusted to dancer-poet, Edwin Denby, recently returned from making a name for himself in Europe, in the belief that he would be able to provide them with something that did not sound like a translation. Denby, as it happens, made a very close translation, only to discover that Welles had quite another — if as yet unexpressed — approach in mind. Welles then joined Denby on the script, and thus began the successful collaboration that was to result in *Horse Eats Hat*. Denby's description of the creative process is most revealing.[2]

"The original period was too tight, too arch. He wanted to avoid all that, and especially too much Gilbertian English which sounded so peculiar to contemporary audiences." Denby agreed, and in the end only the locale remained French. He and Welles had both seen Rene Clair's silent film of *An Italian Straw Hat* and been greatly impressed by it, even though the film was so decidedly French and counter to their own intentions.

Their method of working together was unique:

I would read a speech, and he would criticize it for the sound. If it blurred, he would rephrase it in such a way that the actual spoken sound was very clear and plain and straight. We understood each other perfectly and worked with a good deal of pleasure. Towards the end, when time got pressing, we'd start about 1 A.M. and work all that night and the following day. We wrote two acts at a stretch like that. By the time it got to be two or three the next morning, we were falling asleep alternately. He would say something. I'd write it down and fall asleep. Then, he'd take over and write something. I would wake up and go on from there, while he fell asleep for a moment. We finished at 9 A.M., and he went off to do a radio program.

There was one important point that Denby insisted upon:

The hero shouldn't be farcical in the obvious sense. The French play is very clear about that. The hero is dumb in so many ways that he wins an audience's heart by his charm.

Welles eventually agreed to it.

While still at work on the script, he discovered Joseph Cotton. This was Denby's reaction:

> As soon as I saw him, I knew he was perfect. He had a wonderful sense of humor—and such warmth. It's so easy in farce to forget the warmth, but that's what has to sustain it.

The sense of equal partnership that had sprung up during the collaboration came to an end the very first day of rehearsals:

> I sat in the back of the house watching it. At the end, still thinking we were friends, I called out something or other, some criticism I had in mind. He answered from the stage and put me down completely. Not in a disagreeable way. But it was clear enough to me that, now, he was the director, and that was the end of it.

Horse Eats Hat closely follows the Labiche storyline; both deal with the mayhem that attends the hero's efforts to replace a lady's straw hat that his horse samples while she is dallying in the bushes with a soldier. It is the hero's wedding day, and his father-in-law and the wedding party follow him all over town in his pursuit of a replacement. The very hat finally turns up as one of the wedding presents, and, amidst much confusion, the wayward lady gets it before her husband finds her out.

The setting of the Denby-Welles treatment is still, supposedly, Paris, but everything about it points to rural America. To bring it closer to their audience's frame of reference, the period has been updated from the 1850s to 1908 (or, as W.G.K. of the *New York Sun* reasoned, because the clothes then were "a bit more ridiculous than any that preceeded or followed them").

Horse Eats Hat is peopled with turn-of-the-century Midwesterners rather than nineteenth-century French bourgeoisie. Typical of this metamorphosis is the father of the bride. In *An Italian Straw Hat* he is a horticulturist from the provinces who has agreed to let his daughter marry a wealthy Parisian landlord. In Welles's hands, the obsequious Nonancourt becomes the fiercely independent businessman, Mortimer J. Mugglethorpe, who was almost certainly inspired by his own father, Richard. (Martin Gabel remembers Welles's speaking of his father "as a prototypical American businessman of a kind that is going out of existence."[3] "We may not know what's modish," states Mugglethorpe declaring his credo, "but we know what's right." Likewise, an adjustment has been made in the character of the hero. Fadinand has become Freddie Hopper, a dumb, bumbling, but earnest young man, a projection of what Andy Hardy might well have grown up to be like.

Welles as Mugglethorpe. *Courtesy of Edwin Denby.*

It was understood by everyone who attended *An Italian Straw Hat* exactly what the soldier and his paramour were about underneath the bushes. But Welles, spells it out even more plainly. Fadinand and Freddie both relate finding the adulterous couple. But Freddie does so while changing clothes and, at the appropriate moment, appears with his pants down as if to demonstrate their state of undress.

It is no wonder, then, that so much of the humor in *Horse Eats Hat* was deemed vulgar. The W.P.A. was painfully sensitive to its public image and sent a representative to censor the production. The following day a list of some thirty offenses was delivered to John Houseman, who turned it over to Welles, who passed it down the line to Denby. Its final disposition is unknown. Hiram Sherman, who, as Bobbin, was accountable for more than his share of dirty jokes remembers them as "innocent dirty jokes. It was all a little too free-thinking for the W.P.A." Much of the offending material came in the form of sight gags and, whatever vulgarity there is to be found in the script itself, was obviously compounded by Welles's staging.

One of the first ideas that he conveyed to Denby was that of wanting the horse to come in and eat the hat onstage. Bil Baird, originally called in to make breakaway chairs for the production, was asked if he could design a horse that could actually eat a hat and roller skate. He proceeded to sculpt a clay model (one-twelfth scale) with lines drawn across it to indicate the edges of the pattern. Then he got some "horse cloth," cut out the pieces, and sewed them together. The horse consisted of Welles's assistant and stage manager, Carol King, up front and collaborator Denby as its rear end. The head itself was made of papier-mâché and, with King working the jaw, was able to bite down and swallow the hat.

Thus, before he had even begun work on the text, Welles was thinking ahead to the kind of fantasy life he intended for the production. Its final evolution was to be very much along the lines of a Marx Brothers movie, with wild and improbable acrobatics, with the set and properties becoming all but animate in the confusion.

The horse—with Carol King up front and Edwin Denby in the rear. *Courtesy of Edwin Denby.*

After an overture, the curtain goes up on a mime prologue. The horse enters on roller skates. "A strange beast made, apparently, of an old leopard-cat coat and some odd kitchen utensils, the horse danced, flopped a mean tail, lolled a red tongue and swirled a roguish eye at the audience."[4] This ballet concludes with its eating a straw bonnet that had been hanging from one of the branches of a tree. Freddie appears cracking his whip, and the horse bolts off.

The soldier, Grimshot, and his lady, Agatha, pop up from beneath the tree. Freddie picks up the hat, glances knowingly in their direction, and dashes off after his horse. Donning roller skates, the couple give chase. Blackout.

Act 1 not only provided the usual plot exposition, but established several running gags as well. Uncle Adolph, the family patriarch, arrives with a hat box (his wedding gift) and is followed onstage by his grandson, Augustus, a character for whom there is no equivalent in Labiche's play. Thereafter, Augustus pursues the old man with a wheelchair and contributes to the melee by using both Adolph and the chair as a battering ram.

The setting is Freddie's apartment. An enraged Grimshot subsequently bursts on the scene, his lady in tow, and sets about to wreck everything in sight. Grimshot's prototype was hard on the furniture, but Welles expanded his destructive nature until it became a major point of the play, with furniture breaking and sets collapsing on purpose. Like Harold Lloyd or the Marx Brothers, Freddie, too inhabits a world in which people as well as objects are often unmanageable.

Welles's chief device in *Horse Eats Hat* for drawing his audiences into the events onstage is to have the characters play directly to them. Whether this takes the form of the horse's gesture or one of Freddie's soliloquies, the style is always presentational.

The first act has an ample share of quick exits and entrances, and people popping out of closets at the wrong (i.e., embarrassing) time. But it is only a dim foreshadowing of what is to come. The horse ballet establishes the kind of pictorial fantasy that Welles employs throughout the production.

Much the same note of whimsy introduces act 2. A roller curtain depicts the exterior of Tillie's Millinery Shop. An elderly gentleman in military tunic enters and marches left to right across the stage to music. After exiting he runs around behind the curtain and enters left again. On his second entrance the store front rises, and he is inside the shop. This is Queeper, Welles's equivalent of Tardiveau, the hapless bookkeeper-national guardsman whom the wedding party takes after in the belief that he is, in fact, a justice of the peace.

Beginning with his one-man parade, Queeper is constantly leading some processional or other. Indeed, he even becomes the unwitting leader of the bridal guests, whom Mugglethorpe has marshaled into a kind of bumptious regiment. Their entr'acte routines, together with a skillful use of the curtain (to convey changes of time and scene), dispense with the need for all but one intermission, and prompted the *New Theatre* reviewer to equate Welles's style of production for *Horse Eats Hat* with the screen's use of the fade-out and fade-in.

The millinery shop consists of five doors across a back flat, greatly increasing the number of quick exits and entrances. Freddie arrives to discover that not only is Tillie (an old flame, as he informs the audience) after him, but so, too, are a half-dozen of her Giggling Girls, assistants created for her by Denby and Welles. As if he were not hard-pressed enough to hold his own against Tillie and Grimshot (to say nothing of his future father-in-law), his own body becomes difficult to manage and he usually winds up on his prat.

Throughout the production Welles exploits the contradiction between physical absurdity and rational assurance. Freddie is simply trying to locate a replacement for the Leghorn bonnet that his horse has eaten. His behavior in going about that task, however, both underscores the absurdity of the situation and, inevitably, fosters the confusion.

In act 2 Mugglethorpe and the wedding party blossom in all their glory. They enter the shop in a double line—Mugglethorpe, the general, and his nephew, Bobbin, the drum major—singing

Myrtle's doing it today.
Oh, hurray, hurray, hurray.
This is Myrtle's wedding day.
Oh, hurray, hurray, hurray.

This is to be their marching song. Whenever Mugglethorpe determines to follow Queeper, young Bobbin sounds the pitch, and off they go. Their standard is a rubber plant that Mugglethorpe had potted the day his little girl was born, "And I won't give it up until I give you up."

Nowhere in the play is its style as frankly presentational as with this group; theirs is always a performance within a performance. Mugglethorpe commands them to group:

Bobbin: Uncle, we're grouped.
Muggle: Myrtle, let me tell you about my rubber-plant. Professor. . .

The music begins and he intones his *Father's Lament*. While there is a parallel in *An Italian Straw Hat*, Welles transforms the moment into a vaudeville turn. The bridal party is, quite decidedly, doing its part.

Meanwhile, Freddie has been pumping Tillie for a piece of information, the whereabouts of a replacement for Agatha's hat. No sooner has she provided the address than Joseph, his valet, enters with more bad news. Grimshot has already made short work of several chairs, two bookcases, a coffee table, and a sideboard, and is about to descend on the bric-a-brac. "Go home and throw him out," Freddie orders, "I'm gonna get married." Thinking he means to her, Tillie jumps into his arms, and, together with her Giggling Girls, begins to embrace him. Mugglethorpe reappears and discovers them. "They're my bridesmaids," Freddie offers, by way of explanation. They all set off for the Countess's salon.

Thus far, Welles has built up a series of minor climaxes. Act 3 which follows immediately, is an extravagance of comedy, comprising a phantasmagoria of bizarre happenings and visual spectacle as the curtain falls for the play's only intermission.

As soon as everyone has left the shop, Tillie's roller curtain drops (showing the front of the shop), and Bobbin motors by outside in a cutout automobile, followed by Augustus pushing Uncle Adolph in the wheelchair — and by the horse. Still another curtain comes down, and the rest of the bridal party crosses the stage in their autos, with Myrtle and Mugglethorpe taking up the rear in the wedding car.

After the rather stark settings of the first two acts, the Countess's Salon is overwhelming in its sumptuousness. In the place of multiple doors, it offers a grand piano, a chandelier, and a three-tiered fountain as principle features.

In *An Italian Straw Hat*, the Baroness is first seen in genteel conversation with her cousin. She is an elegant and respectable lady with a penchant for music. In Welles's version she becomes a vain and lecherous hag, who, with her lover Gustave, is first seen stretched out across the fountain seat.

Upon his arrival Freddie is blissfully unaware that the Countess not only thinks him to be Raguso, the Italian tenor she has been expecting, but that she mistakes his eagerness to recover the hat for an expression of manly passion. Everything that Freddie does increases this misunderstanding.

At this point the production achieves heights of fancy that are surrealistic. The Countess has arranged a concert, at which Raguso is to sing a few selections. As her guests begin to arrive, a Butler and Footman step forward to announce them. Starting with the fairly reasonable "Her Royal Highness Helena of Sardinia," they take on an ever-increasing madness, as the Butler and Footman are joined by offstage voices all shouting simultaneously, "The Potentate of Both Petunias," "The White Hope of Turkey," "The Baroda of Burlesque," "The Original Katzenjammers," "The Second Manifesto of Surrealism," "Count Dracula of

Transylvania," and so on. This builds to a great conglomeration of voices and music, and, after the announcement of "Mr. Anthony Adverse. . .The Three Little Pigs. . .The teeth of Gloria Swanson," the remainder of the list is abruptly cut off by a crash of cymbals.

Throughout it all the Countess introduces Freddie to her guests as they enter. Aware now that he is supposed to be the Great Raguso, he turns and bows each time the name is mentioned. The guests pair off and begin dancing. Freddie manages to break away long enough to come down to the footlights for one of his soliloquies: "She thinks I'm Raguso, eh? I'll be Raguso! That's the way to get the hat." Another crash of cymbals, and the guests exit in all directions, leaving Freddie and the Countess alone onstage.

Taking this fixation on a hat to be an appropriate display of temperament for a tenor, she leaves to fetch it for him. A drunken Mugglethorpe enters on tiptoe. The wedding guests have been downstairs playing "tag" and gorging themselves on the Countess's supper, believing it to be laid out for them.

With the bridal party singing "Myrtle's doing it today" just offstage, the Maid enters with a hat—the wrong hat. Freddie goes beserk and tramples it. Grabbing her by the throat, he gets the news that the hat in question belongs, in fact, to a Mrs. Entwhistle. Thereupon, Joseph enters to inform his master what has been happening on the home front.

Joseph is followed by a Prompter, who orders him off the stage, saying, "You don't come into this act." He and the Prompter debate the point. Freddie shouts them down with a plea for Joseph to save the furniture. "Where. . .does. . .she live?" answers the Prompter, reminding Freddie of his correct line. And the play resumes.

Thus, Welles has added to the unreality of the proceedings with this technique of a play within a play. The idea becomes all the more intriguing because he utilizes it only spasmodically. This is the same theatrical device that Thornton Wilder was to fully develop in *Our Town* three years later, and one that Pirandello had already resorted to in the 1920s with *Six Characters in Search of An Author*.

Freddie, the Entwhistle address in his pocket, is about to make good his escape when the Countess and her guests sweep in to hear Raguso's concert. Mugglethorpe has been installed at the piano and starts banging away at it. The wedding party enters riotously to take up the Countess's guests as dancing partners. Bobbin, ever the bandmaster, shouts "Turkey trot! Everybody, turkey trot!" and all those with partners begin to dance.

Bil Baird, who played Augustus, was decked out in a little boy's suit: bare knees, a sailor's blouse, and blonde wig. He enters into the spirit of the scene, propelling Uncle Adolph around the floor, bumping into everyone in sight. He later reported, "They got sore as hell at me. But that was the whole idea; I was there to disrupt the dance."

In the midst of all this confusion, a rotund little man enters. "I am Raguso," he announces. The dancing stops. There is a pause. "It's a fraud!" cries one of the guests. And the mayhem really begins.

Marc Connelly's firsthand observations provide an insight into the actual circumstances of the production. He was aware that this was a W.P.A.-sponsored affair, and credits much of its success to the fact that Welles had a limitless supply of actors available to him. "Everyone who had evening clothes was brought in for the production. A great many of them were seemingly in their eighties, but they were all very lively and having a good time."[5]

Freddie's admission of fraud disconcerts the guests. They reach into their pockets, pull out guns, and begin firing at him. Freddie, in turn, leaps upon the piano, which is then pushed into the center of the stage. He grasps the chandelier and is lifted to a height of about ten feet, where, suspended, the fountain is turned on him. He is then carried away.

Freddie is no sooner out of sight than Queeper and the Night Patrol are rolled in on a moving platform. The entire scene becomes chaotic; even the setting seems to be out of control. Back drapes go up. The front curtain tumbles to the floor. Prop men pick their way through the debris trying to save what they can.

The theatricality of it is like an explosion. This time the play within a play has burst the perimeters of both reality and make-believe. Welles has structured an atmosphere in which the two are indistinguishable.

Finally, six butlers in livery pick their way to the footlights and announce, "Supper is served!" The curtain falls. Whereupon, a lady hussar stands up with her coronet in one of the boxes and proceeds to play. She is not the only divertissement. There are a player piano and a gypsy waltz band, as well. Just before the lights go down for the start of act 4, Bil Baird, in the guise of a drunken spectator, horrifies the audience with a controlled fall from one of the side boxes into the orchestra pit.

One hazard of ending the first part of a production on so high a note is, of course, that what follows tends to be something of an anticlimax. To be sure, Welles had additional tricks up his sleeve, but, theatrically, Part 2 of *Horses Eats Hat* was not nearly so innovative as Part 1. He rounded out the production, and that was about all.

Act 4 begins simply enough at the Entwhistles, with Welles opting for an abrupt change of pace from the earlier goings-on. In effect, he is starting again on a level with act 1. The Entwhistle set is for all intents and purposes, the same as Freddie's apartment, with the center doors being replaced by draw curtains.

The "comedy" here is provided by a bucket in which Agatha's murderous husband is soaking his feet. The bucket is continually being filled with scalding water and is the cause of much stage business.

With the exception of lines changed to keep the spirit of the production, act 4 is the least reconstructed of the play. Only in the final few pages does it again take on the Wellesian touch. Chase music begins. Joseph enters. "Hold Grimshot!" Freddie shouts to him, "Hold that horse marine! Save the fixtures." But, alas, the fixtures are already done for. "Then, save the plumbing," he calls after him, as he dashes off.

Act 5 returns to the visual style established for the play. To the accompanyment of storm music, the wedding party, this time led by Myrtle and Mugglethorpe, enters in their automobiles and remains in a line across the stage. Myrtle raises her umbrella against the rain, and the others follow in one-two-three order. Mugglethorpe has come to reclaim his daughter's trousseau and wedding gifts. With cries of "Back to Bandolia Square!" they turn their autos around and drive off. More rain. Then, Freddie and the horse cross the stage after them, with Entwhistle close on their heels promising, "Blood will be shed this night."

Bandolia Square consists of Freddie's residence on the one side, the police station on the other, and a lamppost between them. The front wall of Freddie's house rises, curtainlike, to disclose a portion of the interior. Grimshot's demolition of the upper front room is now complete, and he can been seen seated among the wreckage meditatively breaking a vase. Outside the police station, Queeper stands watch in a sentinel box.

A few words must be written about Queeper. Denby and Welles's stated intention to retain the charm implicit in *An Italian Straw Hat* was successful not only in the Freddie-Fadinand character, but in their improvisation of Queeper and his friend, Little Berkowitz. Labiche's character, Tardiveau, remains in the National Guard so as to keep the musical duo of himself and Trouillebert together. Queeper, on the other hand, is still a member of the patrol because Little Berkowitz, alias Gumshoe Gus (of the pantry scandal), is in jail, and the only way for them to "keep on their music" is for Queeper to pull guard duty beneath his cell. Thus, Little Berkowitz is revealed playing his tuba behind bars in concert with Queeper on the triangle below.

Freddie appears in the upstairs room of his house to turn the hat box (Uncle Adolph's wedding present) over to Grimshot, who discovers that it is empty and impales it on his sword. By now the night patrol has arrested the wedding party, and as Freddie and Grimshot are discovering the box to be empty, Mugglethorpe appears in the window of a cell wearing the sought-after hat.

Freddie charges to the station. The door flies open and the militia, with bayonets fixed, come out to meet him. Freddie melts before their challenge and throws himself to the ground biting his fingernails. On seeing Grimshot, however, the soldiers present arms and make a double line to the station door through which he walks.

From Mugglethorpe, to Grimshot, to the top of the lamppost — the hat finally winds up (after a momentary blackout) with Agatha, who then berates her husband for ever having doubted her. Freddie and Myrtle come forward to the audience and say: "Well, there you are, ladies and gentlemen, that fixes everything. You can go home now — the play is over."

Immediately, Tillie and her Gorgeous Girls enter and chase Freddie straight into the arms of the Countess and her guests. This final piece of choreography is actually a staged curtain call, culminating in Freddie, Tillie and Myrtle's dancing together, while the rest of the cast line up on either side of them, and atop the roof of the station house several members of the wedding party scatter confetti on the crowd below.

The design of *Horse Eats Hat* was Welles's own, but it fell to Nat Karson to create the costumes, and the gaudy sets, which looked as though they had come from a comic book. To his own costume Welles added so many false items that very little of him was left.

The music for the production was written by Paul Bowles and orchestrated by Virgil Thomson, who remembers it as being a very elaborate score. Actually, Bowles wrote very little music — two pieces of continuity, the horse ballet, and Mugglethorpe's *Lament* — specifically for *Horse Eats Hat*. Thomson has stated that since there was not time to write all the music that was needed, he, as musical director of the project, chose several of Bowles's earlier compositions and adapted them to fit this production. *Modern Music* (November-December 1936) applauded the score, comparing it to "a sur-realistic melange of Satie and Offenbach."

There seems to have been an air of general excitement and anticipation among those who worked on the production. The variety of theatrical effects demanded that all elements work with the absolute precision of a ballet. As he had done on *Macbeth*, Welles again became the master puppeteer. The actors had to time their moves so as to make the whole production flow in a truly farcical manner.

The acting style that Welles brought to this production was modeled along the lines of vaudeville comedy, with a touch of acrobatics thrown in. For example, Joseph Cotton was directed to give a Douglas Fairbanks-like performance. For all his attempts to subordinate his actors, Welles found that he had to depend on them in *Horse Eats Hat*. So, as Edwin Denby put it, "he fed them every line, every inflection. It was like Reinhardt mouthing Schiller." Unfortunately, much of the skill for vaudeville cannot be taught, and certainly not in the course of rehearsals for a production. *Horse Eats Hat* reflected this truism.

The effects he aimed for are clear enough; critical response was, however, divided on whether he achieved them. The daily papers were in the main not impressed. The *Brooklyn Daily Eagle* had this to say the following day:

The authors and directors and the actors work very hard giving the audience broad hints that it is at perfect liberty to laugh. . . .

They know very well what they want to do and they don't know how to do it. . . .This sort of calculated nonsense requires a much sharper calculation than they are equipped to give it. It asks for the expert and there is not a single expert on the premises.

The *New York Sun* found the pace to be too slow, "despite the noise, the mass-rompings and the Keystone-comedy chases." The *New York Times* expressed some pleasure, while wondering about the value of a play that its critic considered meaningless. Its evaluation of audience response seems reasonably correct—"Half. . .was pretty indignant and the other half quite amused." And the *New York Daily News* opened its review with "Wacky—utterly wacky but, paradoxically, not wacky enough." Only the *World-Telegram* was unreservedly friendly.

Yet two months later *New Theatre Magazine* had very kind things to say about the production:

From left to right—Virgil Thomson, Paul Bowles, and Welles as seen from the stage of *Horse Eats Hat. Courtesy of Edwin Denby.*

Welles rehearsing Joseph Cotton as Freddy and Henriette Kaye as Tillie. *Courtesy of the Federal Theatre Project Research Center, George Mason University, Fairfax, Virginia.*

The producers have used the same colorful costume and scenic effects and the efficient manipulation of stage ensemble which helped make *Macbeth* one of the most original productions last year; they have exploited the resources of the theatre and added a few novelties of their own to produce an evening of humorous entertainment.

Marc Connelly, one of the show's most enthusiastic supporters, found himself "laughing like a hyena" in the midst of a generally cool audience. Indeed, the only other laugher turned out to be John Dos Passos. "So, Dos and I sat together during the second half for mutual protection." When asked why so few others responded as he had, Connelly surmised, "They were watching it, rather than sharing in it. They reminded me of what the Greeks called *agelasts*, non-laughers. It's possible, of course, they just weren't attuned to the play."

Despite its generally poor notices, *Horse Eats Hat* enjoyed some rather passionate support. The night of its closing only those who had seen it at least twice were admitted. Martin Gabel, although personally less than amused by "that form of frantic humor," conceded that "the fine arts world—the opera buffs and curators—many of them adored it."

Joseph Wood Krutch's one paragraph review in *The Nation* (October 10, 1936) was the most perceptive:

> The notion of translating the old French farce into surrealist slapstick might have proved amusing had Mr. Welles not elected to submerge it in costume and decor and to stifle the musical score in an obliterating hubbub. . . .In the end the deliberate use of bathos and disorder is no less tiresome for being deliberate, though the venture as a whole is not without flashes of spontaneous fancy.

Welles badly miscast as Andre, the poet-aviator, and Otto Hulett in Sidney Kingsley's ill-fated production of *Ten Million Ghosts* (St. James Theater, October 23, 1936). *Courtesy of Sidney Kingsley.*

4

Doctor Faustus

The feeling prevalent among critics of the Federal Theatre was that its purpose should be to produce plays of timely significance. Viewed in this light, *The Tragical History of Doctor Faustus* was a decided failure. But for anyone interested in the imaginative power of the theatre, the production was a resounding success.

With *Faustus*, Welles managed to turn a rarely produced Elizabethan tragedy into a Broadway hit. This was all the more remarkable because the 1930s was a period that was generally unreceptive to the classics (except for productions of Shakespeare by all-star casts). Welles stated his objectives for *Faustus*: "The aim is to create on modern spectators an effect corresponding to the effect in 1589 when the play was new. We want to rouse the same magical feeling, but we use the methods of our own time."

As Faustus, Welles in effect re-created himself in the image of the master magician. The program notes describe him as one who "must wait patiently till he has passed through all the terrible forms which announce his coming, and only when the last shriek has died away, and every trace of fire and brimstone has disappeared, may he leave the circle and depart for home in safety."

Doctor Faustus appeared at a time when horror movies had whetted the public's sudden appetite for the supernatural. By the mid-thirties *Dracula* and *Frankenstein* had attained the status of popular myths. Together with various other monsters, they provided a thrilling escape for audiences standing on the brink of World War II.

Faustus was presented as the story of just such a monster. He was as forbidding as Frankenstein; however, instead of the usual practice of contrasting mysterious happenings within a recognizable (if often Gothic) setting, Welles created an atmosphere for his production of *Faustus* that was unrecognizable as anything but the background for a magic show.

The images he conjured up were burlesques of horror films. Faustus himself, as he first appeared coming from the back of the stage forward onto the ramp, was very much the movie monster seen not in close-up but as though he were about to step down from the scene into the midst of the audience. Despite his garish makeup, despite his obvious theatricality, Faustus was awe-inspiring because he also bore the import of Marlowe's legendary figure.

Most horror films go to great lengths to create an air of probability. Welles realized that the same emotional ends could be achieved by taking his story in exactly the opposite direction. He presented the character of Dr. Faustus as an obviously and heavily made up impression of himself appearing in a magic act. Then he asked his audience, in effect, to join him in a game of admitted pretense.

The idea for this sort of game may have originated with a play of Welles's own, *Brite Lucifer*. In front of his friend, a young actor dons the costume of "the ghoul." It is obvious to both men how this creature came into being; nevertheless, after putting on his costume the actor becomes, both to himself and to others, "the ghoul."

Welles drastically simplified the original *Doctor Faustus*, following it only through act 3. Afterward, he rearranged lines and whole scenes at will. His own text had fifteen scenes, including two low-comedy scenes compiled from the half-dozen in Marlowe. They were all like magic acts and vaudeville turns presented in the grand guignol manner.

The setting lent a necessary touch of mystery to whatever might happen; it was the perfect working background for a tale of magic. Completely devoid of pictorial detail, the stage was enveloped in black velvet curtains that gave the impression of a dark cavern from which the production emerged. The single object onstage was a black mound (upstage center). Actors made their entrances by "appearing" over the top of the mound or by coming up through traps in the solid black floor.

The stage apron was extended twenty feet into the orchestra. It was constructed especially for the production and was probably one of the first to break out of the proscenium arch in a Broadway playhouse. The larger, ensemble scenes were played in the deeper recesses of the stage, while the soliloquies, low-comedy scenes, and dialogues between Faustus and Mephistopheles took place on the apron—cheek by jowl with the audience. Welles reasoned that such close proximity would cause "the actor to use a larger manner and more voice than when he is separated from his listeners by the proscenium arch. The nearer you are, the bigger you must seem and the louder you must speak, to hold attention." Welles, it seems, foresaw the thrust stage achieving quite the reverse effect from the common use to which it was to be put in the 1950s.

Designer Abe Feder felt that his job, in the absence of scenery, was to find "other means of tying together time and space in the continuity of the script."[1] Since the performance was run without intermission, "the entire burden of changes in tempo and space was placed in the realm of the worker of light. . . .He [Welles] wanted people to appear

Arthur Spencer as Wagner (*right*) and Harry McKee as the Clown in *Dr. Faustus. Courtesy of Edwin Denby.*

and disappear out of the black void." For this reason it was decided to work within a completely black enclosure, and Feder developed what he likens to "the use of light in the third dimension." Stark Young of the *New Republic* (February 17, 1937) took particular note of this effect:

> And Feder. . .has created a body, a dramatic medium, of light, by which the diverse scenes are given, the entrances and exits effected and the dramatic moods established. . . . The settings appear, through the means of light, to be some chiaroscuro of the cosmos. They seem some concentration in space.

The chief means for producing these effects was a row of lights that were hung across the stage. Velvet cones extended from the bottom of the lights to just above the proscenium arch (a distance of about twenty feet). The audience thus saw only solid columns of light formed by the controlled beams hitting the dust in the air. Characters upstage of the beams would, therefore, be invisible until they were caught by their light.

Drawing upon an old Chinese system (one still commonly used by puppeteers the world over), objects were made to disappear in much the same way. Stagehands dressed all in black were lost against the cyclorama. They carried quarter-inch rods, six feet in length. The rods were attached to the object that was to disappear. At the appropriate cue, the stagehands would swing the objects up behind them and out of sight.

There is no telling who was actually responsible for the creation of these effects, Welles or Feder. Bil Baird has said that Welles "had a tendency to absorb credit for anything like that." Publicly, Welles acknowledged as to how Feder had arranged the lighting cues and orchestrated the men at the switchboards. An educated guess is that, being a longtime student of magic, he (Welles) knew the effects that he wanted; and Feder, a master of lighting technique, realized them for him. Despite the success of collaboration, it was not a happy one, and Feder has been unwilling to discuss anything beyond the technical details of their work together.

There were seventy-six major lighting cues and sound effects in the production, each of which had a number of subdivisions. At one point there were so many lights hung from the grid that it broke under the weight, and the cast had to abandon the Maxine Elliott Theatre for nearly a week while repairs were being made. Though the effect worked well, it could hardly have been under anything even resembling pleasant working conditions for either Feder or Welles.

Because of his experience as a radio actor and (soon-to-be) director, Welles was acutely aware of the dramatic possibilities of sound. A public address system was installed that piped the special effects throughout the theatre.

A good many of the forty-five actors in the production were used solely as off-stage voices. In addition to the voices and electronic effects, the production featured an old-fashioned thunder drum. This has been described by Bil Baird:

> Here was one of the biggest goddammed bull-skins you can imagine. They stretched it wet over a frame made of four-by-tens. It was so strong that it pulled the corners of the frame apart. But you never heard a thunder drum like that. You never did. It was banging over on Stage Right up about four feet off the floor. All you had to do was take a hammer and just touch it, and you got a sound that went all through the theatre. You could even feel it in your seat.

This impressed Welles's CBS colleagues who were beside themselves with praise over his innovative use of sound. However, their reaction was not shared uniformly by the critical fraternity.

The curtain for *Doctor Faustus* was usually around nine. It was down again by ten fifteen. There was no intermission because, as Hiram Sherman tells us, "the acts would have been less than a half-hour long." One evening there was a movie that Welles wanted to go to. So, according to Sherman, he urged his cast to "play it for the record books. The audience was back out on the streets before they'd hardly gotten settled in their seats, and Orson was off and away to the Paramount [Theatre] to catch his movie."

Welles might be pardoned for his somewhat self-indulgent approach to performance. Not only did he direct *Faustus*, but, as its leading man, he was onstage almost continuously. In addition, he was a busy radio actor appearing in two broadcasts, one at 8 P.M. and the other at 8:30. He thus had to do some fast traveling to meet *Faustus*'s nine o'clock curtain. Welles described the situation as follows:

> I go to the studio in my Faustus make-up, beard and all, and wearing a tuxedo. . . .The sketches are arranged so that I say my last speech a few minutes before 9. Then I jump into the taxi. The chorus has the opening scene in *Faustus*, and while that is going on I am getting into my costume.

The acting in *Faustus* met with mixed approval. The critics who deplored the production were particularly dissatisfied. Wilella Waldorf of the *New York Post* expressed the general reaction: "Marlowe's work, if it must be produced at all in the modern theatre, should be well spoken, and that is something the actors corralled by Unit 891 are not up to."

Welles's concept of production in general tended to ignore the importance of individual performances, with his interest focused largely on the total scheme. As a result, the quality of the acting was often neglected, except for the stylistic details that he could drill into his cast. John Houseman has said that *Faustus* "gave a unified and vivid impression of Welles' very special theatrical talent." This much can be accepted as truth. As for the acting being a part of this unity, however, there is considerable doubt. Edith Isaacs of *Theatre Arts* (February 1937) thought that the production was creative and successful in both idea and achievement, but found the acting so bad that she declined to comment further on it. Stark Young was kind. He called the acting adequate and noted that he, at least, had no particular difficulty in hearing the lines.

However little attention he may have paid to his actors, at least one of them, Hiram Sherman, trusted him. The following episode, told by Sherman, is typical of what Welles could do.

One night I had to go on as one of the comics. I had to enter by coming up through a trap that led out of the orchestra pit. The night I had to go on, the one thing I didn't know was when, although we'd rehearsed the scene. I was in the middle of the orchestra — fiddles to the right of me, fiddles to the left of me — on a ladder. I could barely hear what was going on over the trap. I said, "My God, I don't know when to go on!" Orson said, "Wait a minute, Chubby. Something happens, you'll know." I said, "what happens?" "I don't know," was the reply, "but don't worry about it. Something will happen." And suddenly the hottest spot situated under the ladder came on. Orson said, "that's it!" And I pushed open the trap and went on. It was a nice effect with the light showing out.

In describing his faith in his direction, Sherman inadvertently reveals something of Welles's methods. The effect, after all, was the important thing.

Welles himself appeared in the title role. Contemporary comment indicates that he was not entirely prepared for it — relying, as he often did, on his natural authority to get him by. Stark Young said that Welles might in time be able to recite verse, as he already had the gift of projecting his voice. But he saw no reason why Faustus had to be mussed and grimy instead of being suave, distinguished, and discriminating. For Wilella Waldorf, Welles "not only chewed up Marlowe's words with the frenzy of a madman but swallowed them before our very eyes."[2] And Edith Isaacs found him entirely unfitted for the role, despite his keen intelligence.

On the other hand, Jack Carter as Mephistopheles was generally well received. He appeared on stage looking like a fallen angel, his face and bald head gleaming against the black background. Many critics referred to him as "the Negro actor," but no one felt that his race made the casting inappropriate. His performance did, however, stir some controversy among those who held to a different view of what the devil's emissary ought

Welles as Faustus. *Courtesy of Hortense and Roger Hill.*

Jack Carter as a scowling Mephistopheles looks on as Faustus
signs his pact with the Devil. *Courtesy of Hortense and Roger
Hill.*

to be like. *Variety* found his concept of the role tempered with human understanding. So, too did Stark Young of *New Republic* adding: "Mr. Jack Carter as Mephistopheles brings something to the part that the ordinary actor of the rant school might miss." But the *Brooklyn Daily Eagle* dismissed his performance in a single word — "colorless!"

Although his production was very much an original work, Welles felt it incumbent upon himself to justify what he had done with Marlowe. He reasoned that unlike the Chinese or the French, the English theatre had no traditional way of performing its classics; thus, each great work had to be produced, and make its impact, in its own way.

Welles's *Doctor Faustus* was primarily a piece of innovative theatrical intelligence and, for many, seemed to be a fresh and ingenious production, one that meant something in terms of the American theatre. Edith Isaacs commented that its success was an indication of how the professional theatre had lost an eager audience. *Commonweal* (January 22, 1937) praised the Federal Theatre Project, calling *Doctor Faustus* "a welcome relief from realism and propaganda."

There were, however, taxpayers and pressure groups that remained steadfastly unreconciled with anything that smacked of the New Deal. Gilbert Gabriel of the *New York American* considered the production pretentious and empty, finding all of Welles's techniques — both in lighting and in sound — to be arty and ineffective. The impartiality of this criticism is somewhat suspect in light of Gabriel's comment about being generous toward the government as a play producer.

Welles had set out to startle his audience, and startle it he did. He did not give the audience time to discover whether he was using comedy as a foil to tragedy or tragedy as a foil to comedy. The images he created were beyond the realm of reality and so impressed the public that the play became a great success. In fact, such a success that ticket scalpers ran the prices up from the federal ceiling of eighty-nine cents to over two dollars.

Despite the critics, the play ran for sixteen weeks. And that, for a play more than three hundred years old, was quite a record.

5
The Cradle Will Rock:
A Comment

Welles's productions for the Federal Theatre had succeeded in making Elizabethan tragedy and nineteenth-century French boulevard farce popular entertainments for his audiences. There were noticeably fewer objections to his alterations of the texts and radical staging practices than usually confront the sort of license he took. This was due, in the main, to his very popularity. Derived as they were from "serious" theatrical traditions, Welles's productions had about them the stamp of "high art," while still managing to engage their audiences in ways that neither the commercial theatre nor the avant-garde were able to.

Welles was the beneficiary of a cultural phenomenon. In the 1930s aesthetic and political judgments merged to form a new Popular Front culture. Possibly more than at any other time in American history, the intelligentsia came to sympathize with the working masses of America, and the art they supported had first to conform with their liberal politics. For Robert Warshow this constituted nothing less than a "disasterous [*sic*] vulgarization" of the very tenets of intellectual life. "A poet [Archibald MacLeish] became Librarian of Congress and denounced American intellectuals for weakening their country's spirit. *The Grapes of Wrath* was a great novel. . .and "Ballad for Americans" an inspired song."[1] Culture of the "middle-brow" had come into being.

In April 1937 Welles went outside the WPA to stage the Aaron Copland-Edwin Denby opera for children, *The Second Hurricane*, at the Henry Street Playhouse. He surrounded the playing area with a Parents' Chorus (*right*), a Pupils' Chorus (*left*), and conductor Lehman Engel and the orchestra (*rear*). *Courtesy of Lehman Engel.*

These same people made up a sizable part of Welles's audience at the Federal Theatre. Houseman reveals that an even larger part of his audience was drawn from the leftwing, particularly members and followers of the Communist Party. It was to woo this group that Houseman and Welles decided to produce Marc Blitzstein's labor opera, *The Cradle Will Rock*. They were thinking ahead, beyond the Federal Theatre, to the launching of their own Mercury Theatre, and communist support meant the guarantee of an audience.

In a 1972 television interview Houseman maintained that there was no political motive behind the decision to produce *The Cradle Will Rock*; he and Welles "just wanted to put on an exciting show." The fact is, they had already decided to break away from the Federal Theatre and, in doing so, turned for support to the only theatrical audience then available to them — the organized left.

It took no remarkable political insight to recognize that *The Cradle Will Rock*, championing as it does the aims of radical labor, would meet with resistance from the Washington bureaucracy. Between their announcement to produce *The Cradle* in March and its scheduled opening in June, political support for the Federal Theatre Project had suffered a good deal of erosion. In an attempt to hold off the Project's opponents, Hallie Flanagan, its national director, arranged for an official government censor to attend a run-through of *The Cradle*. Instead of the expected opposition to the show," the man from Washington pronounced it "Magnificent!"

By alienating Washington, Houseman and Welles had hoped to improve their standing with the left-wing faction of their audience. After the "Voodoo" *Macbeth, Horse Eats Hat*, and *Dr. Faustus*, something more relevant to the current political scene was definitely in order—a labor opera, for example. Thus, the censor's favorable verdict on *Cradle* proved a decided liability, not simply for this production but for Houseman and Welles's own future plans. The government itself resolved their dilemma. On June 12, four days before *The Cradle* was to open, a memorandum was sent out to all project heads prohibiting, for budgetery reasons, the opening of any cultural event before July. Houseman and Welles, pouncing on this sudden opportunity, reacted to the memo as if it had been directed against *The Cradle* alone, and they flatly refused to postpone the production. Although delays of two weeks and more in opening their production were already a commonplace for Houseman and Welles, in the case of *The Cradle* they became, in Houseman's words, "demons of dependability, scrupulous to honor our public and artistic committment."[2] Flanagan tried to intervene in their behalf but was told by Washington that there could be no exceptions to the ruling. Whereupon Welles, with Archibald MacLeish in tow arranged a meeting with the W.P.A. administration. They were told that the show was postponed—not canceled. Washington made it clear that were Houseman and Welles to go outside the auspices of the Federal Theatre to open *Cradle*, they would withdraw all future support for the production. What these events demonstrate, above all else, is that Houseman and Welles managed to turn a rather routine government directive into an act of official censorship. That, of course, only served to bolster their image as radical producers.

On June 14 they forced the government's hand and announced a special preview of *The Cradle* at the Maxine Elliott Theatre for an invited audience. In attendance for that performance was the usual smattering of Broadway luminaries, a large contingent from the Worker's Alliance, and V. J. Jerome, cultural czar of the Communist Party in America. That audience, according to Houseman, "was the only one that ever saw and heard Marc's work performed as he wrote it." The next day federal officers padlocked the theatre.

In reconstructing that performance, from Houseman's memoirs and

from interviews with participants and bystanders alike, one is struck by
the fact that Welles and his designer on *The Cradle*, Edward Shruers,
had devised a production scheme for Blitzstein's proletarian opera that
can best be described as "extravagant." Blitzstein, who claimed Brecht
and Weill as his inspiration (their *Mahagonny*, in particular), seems not
to have realized that what Houseman described as "the rising theatrical
excitement that was being generated on our own bare, worklit stage"
during rehearsals of *The Cradle* could but be dissipated by the spectacle
that Welles had planned for its production.

Only after Houseman and Welles had been locked out of the Maxine
Elliott and their costumes and scenery confiscated were they, in effect, in
the position that the Communist Party prescribes for workers' theatre.
The *Dram Buro Report* for May of 1932 declared that the structure of
revolutionary theatre, its choice of plays, and staging methods "must be
such that we are able to travel with our production from one place to
another, that we are able to give the same effective performance on a stage,
on a bare platform, on the street."[3] Thus, the conditions under which
Houseman and Welles finally opened *The Cradle Will Rock* at the Venice
Theater on June 16 were, in fact, ideal.

The musicians union, which was affiliated with the American
Federation of Labor, regarded *Cradle* as CIO propaganda and would not
permit its members to work the show. Likewise, the actors were enjoined
by their union from appearing on stage in this production for any
management other than the Federal Theatre. This was more adversity
than Houseman and Welles had anticipated, but even these problems
turned out to work to their advantage.

The Downtown School of Music had bought out opening night, and,
on Houseman's assurance that there would indeed be a performance,
they refused to surrender their tickets. First the press, then the audience,
began to assemble outside the Maxine Elliott Theatre that evening.
Shortly before eight o'clock, several members of the cast came forward
and offered a sort of sidewalk preview of *The Cradle*. All the while this
was going on, Houseman and Welles were holed up inside, supposedly
scouring the city for another theatre. Bil Baird, who helped to load the
piano aboard the flatbed truck for the trip uptown still maintains that the
long delay in letting the crowd know that they had secured the Venice
Theatre was more for theatrical effect than a matter of necessity, and
that the plethora of stories that have been spawned by this event are
simply "embroidery."

Finally, it was announced that *Cradle* would open at nine o'clock
at the Venice Theater. "There was," as Houseman tells us, "a strong
smell of history in the air." In retrospect, it would appear that he and
Welles were about the business of mythmaking. Cast and audience alike
surrendered themselves to it and trekked uptown. At the Venice they

Sketches by Edward Schruers for the "extravagant" production of *The Cradle Will Rock. Courtesy of Lehman Engel.*

had to wait for the house crew, which was assembled very quickly, if, as Houseman would have us believe, the theater had been empty barely an hour before their arrival. Promptly at nine he introduced himself to the overflow audience ("sincerely but ingenuously"), telling them that "as artists and men of the theatre we had no choice but to defy" the government's arbitrary and unjust directive that they were not to open a production that they knew to have reached "the stage of readiness when it must be shared with an audience."[4] What they shared was Marc Blitzstein alone at the piano on an empty stage, and actors delivering their lines from orchestra seats, from the boxes, from the balcony, everywhere but from the stage (thus carrying out the mandate from their union). It was an electrifying performance and drew national headlines.

The Cradle was, as Hallie Flanagan later wrote, a springboard for publicity for Houseman and Welles, who ask us to believe that in putting it on they were only keeping their word to their audience. In severing their ties with the Federal Theatre, Houseman and Welles acquired with the production of The Cradle Will Rock what must have seemed to them at the time a much more durable patron.*

---

*Shortly after the Mercury Theatre opened, Houseman and Welles showed fealty by reviving The Cradle on Sundays for a month. Afterward they turned Sundays, their dark night, over to the New Theatre League. Among the plays produced under their aegis were Ben Bengal's labor comedy, Plant in the Sun, and The Bishop of Munster, a monologue by H. S. Kraft that featured Morris Carnovsky. It is interesting to note that within a year Houseman and Welles became disenchanted with the left and broke with them to enter the orbit of the Theatre Guild.

Marc Blitzstein rehearses the cast of *The Cradle. Courtesy of the Federal Theatre Project Research Center, George Mason University, Fairfax, Virginia.*

6

Julius Caesar

"It was the definitive Mercury production in its supreme theatricality."
Such is Norman Lloyd's memory of *Julius Caesar* and, in fact, no Welles
production before it (not even *Faustus*) or afterward succeeded so completely in meshing his own staging techniques with the taste and desires
of his audience. *Caesar* was unquestionably Welles's highest achievement
in the theatre.

One of the principle factors that made it so was his audience's
acute sensibility to the threat of fascism. By emphasizing this consideration,
Welles was able to establish a resemblance between republican Rome and
fascist Italy in the most obvious visual terms. He then made certain that
any further parallels would not only be perceived but anticipated. Caesar
became the archtypal dictator; Brutus, the idealistic liberal; Cassius, the
calculating revolutionary; and the citizens of Rome, the gullible hordes
that were even then donning armbands and the other insignia of fascism
to follow Hitler and Mussolini.

Indeed, a number of reviewers were so caught up in their enthusiasm
for these parallels that they failed to notice that they were entirely of
Welles's own making. *Julius Caesar* proved so timely and provocative
that the critics were actually arguing whether Shakespeare favored
fascism or communism, or possibly that he was a Trotskyite.

While intending an unmistakable reference to Italian despotism,
Welles did not dress his conspirators and storm troopers in black shirts
or brown. Because of the emotional appeal, which was derived from the
contemporary parallel (the physical resemblance to Mussolini of Joseph
Holland playing Caesar), audiences were able to suppose that the play
itself was a worthy antifascist tract.

The difference between Shakespeare and Welles is clear; Shakespeare
was primarily interested in character, Welles in action. Shakespeare's
objections to Caesar stem mainly from his being a usurper and personally
unworthy of his ambitions. Shakespeare was, after all, an exponent of
monarchy—so long as the proper order of succession was maintained.

Caesar's assassination proves that the overthrow of any ruler, however poor or inept he may be, generally leads to disaster for all.

Welles's text greatly altered the original; even so, he was unable to make it any more anti-fascist than Shakespeare had. The concept of his production was complete and coherent; however, the mood he imbued it with was so rooted in contemporary state politics that the logic of the text came into question. Caesar is assassinated because he is personally ambitious; but then it appears that Caesar was a benevolent dictator and that his assassins have committed a grievous wrong. The parallels with Mussolini should not be stressed too closely.

Julius Caesar was a dazzling piece of propaganda, with the political equation so skillfully drawn that the spectator could not help but be partisan. Welles resorted to the basic vocabulary of his time against war and fascism, and re-created Shakespeare's play in such familiar visual terms as to obviate the need for contemporary dialogue. (Who in the audience could fail to believe that Caesar was anything but evil when he looked so strikingly like Mussolini?) The highest form of propaganda utilizes the emotive and connotative power of imagery and symbols. It is this sense that Welles created his *Caesar*, giving a new vitality to an old history and making it timely.

Welles by no means exhausted the resources of his material; rather, he shaped both the play and its characters into a story of action. The length of the performance, reduced to something just over an hour and one-half, required a certain amount of rearranging and a great deal of cutting. His methods of editing were much the same as those he had used previously for *Macbeth*. Scenes and characters were slanted to make only the points he wanted them to make. Soliloquies were either sharply pared or converted into dialogues (like Cassius's musings at the end of Act 1, scene 2, which Welles rewrote as an exchange between Casca and Cassius).

Welles also continued his practice of "borrowing"; a character's lines might be given to someone else, or a block of dialogue transposed from one scene to another. Here, too, he even went so far as to borrow from elsewhere in Shakespeare—notably, from *Coriolanus*. ("The other side of the city is risen./Why stand we here?" is one such example. Welles added these lines to the Cinna the Poet scene.) If Welles needed a line to get somebody offstage, or to end a scene, and it was not supplied by *Julius Caesar*, he would, in effect, say, "Wait a minute! There's a line in. . ." and put it into the script.

Generally speaking, however, there was not too much improvising of that sort. Welles was, by all reports, prepared to do *Caesar* (if not as fully prepared as John Houseman maintains). He had acted in (playing both Cassius *and* Mark Antony), designed, and had a hand in the direction of a bare-stage production of it at the Todd School, and his later script required few alterations.

During rehearsals *Julius Caesar* was performed both with and without an intermission until, finally, Welles decided it was better if done uninterrupted. This idea of an unbroken continuity evidently appealed to Welles. He had already used it with *Dr. Faustus* and would do so again with *The Shoemaker's Holiday* and *Danton's Death*.

Welles's narrative followed Shakespeare rather closely through the third act, with only act 3, scene 4 omitted in its entirety. To be sure, there were numerous cuts, as well as rearrangements of dialogue; but the plot was not substantively changed.

After the Cinna the Poet scene, however, Welles turned his hand to a more radical alteration of the text. He elected to show the aftermath of the assassination solely from the conspirators' vantage. He has Cassius and Brutus quarreling about their plans, but upon learning of their enemies' advance, agreeing to meet at Phillipi. Act 4 is thus compressed greatly — but not nearly so much as act 5, which consists of a single page in Welles's version. Brutus receives news of Antony's victory (actually, Pindar's faulty report in act 5, scene 3), gazes down on upon Cassius's body (slain by enemies in Welles's text), and mourns his death. The lights dim momentarily for his own suicide, and rise again for Antony to speak his brief regrets over him, the noblest Roman, as the play ends.

Audiences entering the Mercury Theatre were confronted with the pitted brick wall of the stage, and with the steampipes clearly visible, as was a New York City fireman whose presence was required by local ordinance. In addition to the heating apparatus, a pair of flag poles reared up the sides of the proscenium. (While not put to any use, they could not be dismantled.) Only the curtain was removed. The stage wall, painted the color of dried blood, was itself a striking image in the production.

Except for an arrangement of wooden platforms, the stage proper was bare. A ramp began at the back wall and rose to the highest level, which was midway between the front and rear of the stage. This had the effect of tilting the stage *away* from the audience (a reverse of the usual raked stage). Welles thus contrived to give the tiny Mercury the appearance of having space, and so enlarged the scope of his entire production, achieving the unimpeded freedom of an Elizabethan stage.

Columns of light picked out the actors, emphasized the action and moods, and established the atmosphere of the various scenes. This was essentially the same method employed earlier in the year with *Dr. Faustus*. The variety of effects that light had created in *Faustus* were increased in the production of *Julius Caesar*. Thus, when Brutus speaks at Caesar's funeral, lights form a cross with Brutus at the center. For Antony, however, the ominous Nuremberg effect was used. Nor did actors exit through doors or into the wings; they were simply blotted out by darkness.

It is impossible to distinguish between the pure theatricality of *Julius Caesar* and the effectiveness of its propaganda. The impression one gets is that many of the effects were found so thrilling because the message they dramatized was one that the audience was entirely sympathetic with. The Elizabethan mob was accepted by the New York audience as coming from contemporary headlines.

It would be fruitless to describe Welles's *Caesar* as an updated, melodramatized version of Shakespeare. Despite the textual similarities, his method of production was itself enough to qualify it as a new work. Not only was emphasis less on character than on the flood tide of revolution swirling throughout the streets, but the story that was most visible (and provocative) was of Welles's own making. Audiences knew that they were supposedly seeing a play that took place in ancient Rome. However, their emotional reaction was quite something else again.

The production begins with Caesar, dressed in a green uniform, scowling behind the masklike face of a modern dictator. His first gesture is a fascist salute that the others returned. From the outset, therefore, it is clear that this Caesar is meant to be more of a symbol than a man. Joseph Holland was the reckless, swaggering, self-confident dictator with the stride of importance. His costume was the type of uniform effected by a Hitler or a Mussolini, but it was Holland's uncanny resemblance to Il Duce, both in manner and appearance, that defined him so exactly. Actually, there was no insignia on the uniforms whatsoever. They were all the same dark olive green in color.

The street dress worn by the crowds was dominated by military garb, Sam Browne belts, epaulettes, and boots. All this may have been modern dress, but as one critic rightly observed, it was still in costume. Not enough costume, however, for Millia Davenport, who later became the Mercury's principal designer. She flatly refused to have anything to do with this production, saying, "Let somebody else dye all those uniforms!"[1]

Casca, Decius Brutus, Legarius, and Trebonius—all the petty conspirators—were portrayed as modern day racketeers with turned-up collars, black hats pulled low around their ears, and that gun-in-the-pocket look about them. As emissaries of the state, both Publius and Mark Antony wore soldiers' tunics, while Brutus, on the other hand, wore a formal mufti, not unlike the kind that might be worn at an afternoon wedding.

The Mercury *Caesar* was a play of action carried along by its patterns of movement. Through men and lights alone, Welles created scenes of terror and power. He may have shown himself to be a briliant innovator in his deployment of the principals, but it was his meticulous orchestration of the crowd scenes that drummed the play's meaning into the minds of his audience. And he did it by the noise of his mobs as they prowled about, herdlike, in the shadows.

Joseph Holland as Caesar receiving the fascist salute. Welles as Brutus is closest to him. Joseph Cotton as Publius is at the far left. Third from the left is Martin Gabel as Cassius. *Courtesy of Walter Ash.*

The more successful scenes were those involving mass movement, and these played with electric quickness. Perhaps because Welles's method was essentially opposed to individualism, the action slackened when the play turned to more intimate scenes.

There is no doubt that Welles was his most resourceful when he could exercise dictatorial control over the ensemble and the scenic effects. The crowning instance of this was the assassination scene itself. Here the visual elements were fashioned after choreographic abstractions to give a stage picture of overwhelming consequence and theatricality.

The conspirators are positioned in a diagonal line across the stage. Caesar, rolling from one to another in a kind of broken-field run, is, in turn, stabbed by each of them. Finally, he reaches downstage. There is only one person left to run to—Brutus, standing like a column against the proscenium wall. His knees buckling, Caesar turns to him as his final haven of safety. Without a word Brutus's hand comes out of his overcoat pocket, and he stands there clutching a knife while Caesar hangs on to his lapels. The enormous figure of Brutus gives no ground to the cringing Caesar, whose face registers the question—will he save me? Caesar's own answer, barely audible, is one of absolute resignation: "Et tu Brute? Then fall Caesar." The knife goes in and Caesar slumps to the ground. It was more climactic than the most piercing scream, for when Caesar finally spoke it was simply to verbalize the statement that the entire scene had already made.

Welles began to build up to this moment in the previous scene with Calpurnia, where he developed the sense that the very people Caesar took to be his allies were the ones who were actually trying to kill him. Thereafter, every moment was charged with that special irony, so that by the time Caesar confronts Brutus the tension had risen to an electrifying peak.

Likewise, the assassination scene demonstrated the bare bones of Welles's theatrical vocabulary for this play. The climax occurs at the moment of greatest contrast between the rising intensity of the visual and the falling off of the vocal. Welles did exactly the opposite of what was expected and, as the result, achieved twice the effect. Action, tempo, mood, and movement—all joined into a sense of utter inevitability.

As an artistic strategy this was neither concealed nor subtle. Indeed, the theatrical effect that Welles sought was always a bold and primitive one. However, that in itself suggested a kind of subtlety that transcended the rather obvious statement around which he had arranged the production.

Meanwhile, another facet of his nature crept through. Along with everyone else in the cast, he was supplied with a rubber dagger to use in the assassination scene. Welles, however, developed a great antipathy to this stageprop and, instead, chose for himself a bone-handled hunting knife, which nightly he would thrust under Caesar's arm. One night, he severed an artery and in the blackout Joseph Holland had to be carried offstage and rushed to the hospital. When the lights came up again for the Cinna the Poet scene, Norman Lloyd found himself sloshing around in blood. There was, of course, a good deal of publicity over the incident, none of which made Welles entirely unhappy. "It was all grist for his mill," reasoned Hiram Sherman.

The idea of subtitling his production "The Death of a Dictator" may have originated as a promotional gimmick, but Welles's imagination carried it far beyond that. Still, it was inevitable that the more publicized scenes were those which represented the analogy between Caesar's world and a fascist society. To be sure, Welles was not out to make any bold political statement; indeed, the very ground note of the production was his audience's own superstitions about dictatorships. These could be traced to the influence of movie newsreels and popular magazines. Welles, in turn, endowed them with theatrical impact—so much so that one is tempted to compare elements of the production to comic-strip versions of dictatorship. Nevertheless, this is precisely what impressed both critics and audiences alike.

Following Caesar's murder the staging reached its climax. There have been very few more thrilling stage pictures than the funeral orations of Brutus and Antony, and they completely justified Welles's simplicity of production.

The development of this scene was described by the late Jean Rosenthal in her memoirs:

> Orson dictated clearly and exactly the look he wanted. . .a very simple look based on the Nazi rallies at Nuremburg. The pattern implied in the Nuremburg "festivals" were in terms of platforms, which were the basis of the scenery, and lights which went up and down. The up light was taken entirely from the effect the Nazis achieved.[2]

When the lights rose for the funeral orations, they revealed a high pulpit (rolled in on casters) around which a crowd had gathered. As Octavius does not figure into Welles's text, the clear implication is that Antony has become Caesar's heir. In his maneuverings to firm up his claim, even the "Friends, Romans, Countrymen" speech sounded like a rabble-rousing harangue.

Stark Young, writing in the *New Republic* (December 1, 1937), noticed this sense of pointed emphasis in the stress Welles placed on individual incident. Yet Young was offended by the production's excesses of theatricality, pointing out that in many spots Welles's technique was all too obvious.

The orations were made over Caesar's body, which should have necessitated Joseph Holland's lying in state for the duration of the third act. To avoid this a young boy disguised with Holland's death mask filled in for him. Bil Baird, who fashioned it out of plaster, at first supposed that it was to be worn by a dummy. Only afer he brought it around to the Mercury was he told by Jean Rosenthal, "We can't afford a dummy. We've got to use a kid." Baird then recast the mask, this time in papier-mâché with several holes for breathing.

Of all the many scenes in the play, the Cinna the Poet scene was, perhaps, nearest to the fundamental image of dictatorships. Welles took Shakespeare's short relief scene, built it up with lines from Coriolanus, added some business of his own, and turned it into a cynical, horror-filled commentary on the mob. The enlargement of the Cinna scene served to further reinforce Welles's statement made earlier in the funeral scene—that

A sketch by Welles from the *Everybody's Shakespeare* edition of *Julius Caesar,* which anticipates the cross-of-light effect that he used in the Mercury production when Brutus speaks at Caesar's funeral. . .*Courtesy of Hortense and Roger Hill.*

. . .but for Antony (George Coulouris) the sinister Nuremberg effect was used. *Courtesy of Walter Ash.*

the source of a dictator's strength must lie in the people from whom he emerges.

The Cinna the Poet scene was, for Joseph Wood Krutch of *The Nation* (November 27, 1937), "an unforgettably sinister thing"; Stark Young of the *New Republic* (December 1, 1937) called it "a piece of creative theatre innovation that is brilliant, even dazzling"; while Grenville Vernon of *Commonweal* (December 3, 1937) said that it was "a scene which for power and sinister meaning has never been surpassed in the American theatre."

However memorable, the scene itself was, by all accounts, only realized after a great amount of wasted effort. There were several false starts; then Welles stopped rehearsing it altogether for nearly three weeks. Instead, he devoted himself to piecing together a sound track (with the help of Irving Reis, his producer on *The Shadow*) that was intended to heighten the scene. However, all this did was garble the scene, and the track was finally eliminated.

Norman Lloyd compounded the problem by his disagreement with Welles over how the character of Cinna should be played. Welles envisioned him in the Byronic tradition, while Lloyd's ideas were along the lines of "a street poet, his pockets bulging with verse."

Welles turned the scene over to Marc Blitzstein, who, with a metronome, devised an accelerating rhythmic pattern to build up the rising menace. But that also failed to resolve matters. Less than forty-eight hours before opening Welles, in desperation, accepted Lloyd's notion of Cinna and staged the scene around that character. The scene began to work, and the next morning it was announced that the Cinna the Poet scene would be in the show for the matinee.

Without it, Welles had found himself confronted with a gaping hole in the structure of the play, as the first set of previews clearly pointed out. After its reinstatement, however, the Cinna the Poet scene, coming as it did in the wake of Antony's incitement of the mob, emerged as the fulcrum around which the entire production revolved.

The opening concept of the scene was pantomimic, and had about it a deceptively quiet—even comic—air. Lloyd (as Cinna) the oblivious victim, meanders into a pool of light. "I dreamt tonight that I did feast with Caesar,. . ." he muses wistfully. Then, without warning, the crowd is upon him—singly, then in twos and threes, coming out of the surrounding darkness until it forms a ring around him. Cinna, assuming they have come for his verses, begins to fish them out of his pockets. Quickly the mood changes as they press in around him with their questions: "What is your name?" "Whither are you going?" "Where do you dwell?" "Are you a married man or a bachelor?"

Arthur Anderson, who played the boy, Lucius, remembers Lloyd's performance with the deepest admiration. While admittedly guessing at

Lloyd's motivation, the sense of it, Anderson feels, was that of Cinna saying to himself: "This isn't happening to me. They're playing a joke on me. Oh, you think I'm Cinna the Conspirator! But I'm not. I'm Cinna the Poet, fellas!"[3]

From offstage a chorus of extras takes up the chant:

Come. Kill. Ho. Slay.
Come. Kill. Ho. Slay.
To the Capitol.
To the Capitol.

The mob closing in on Norman Lloyd as Cinna the Poet.
Courtesy of Walter Ash.

Cinna, by now wide-eyed and cringing, offers samples of his poems to the mob around him, only to have them wadded up and thrown back into his face. One step at a time, they converge on Cinna. From out of the shadows comes the pronouncement, "Tear him for his bad verses!" Cinna, backing away, turns from one to the other imploringly, "I'm Cinna the Poet, not Cinna the Conspirator." At this point the mob's ranks are doubled with extras and, together, they swallow him up. Blackout. Silence. Then, a last frenzied cry—"BUT I'M CINNA THE POET!" This is followed by the peal of a Hammond organ struck full volume on all the bass keys and pedals for what seems like minutes (but is actually forty-five seconds). As Martin Gabel put it, "Welles's genius showed itself most clearly in his ability to build up fundamentally minimal situations so effectively."

The funeral orations had been so orchestrated as to unleash the climactic fury that descended on the hapless poet. Antony, standing with arms raised in the fascist salute, had whipped the mob into the emotional maelstrom that led to Cinna's murder. The cumulative effect of virulence and brutality was exploited by Welles to reveal in this single moment the legacy of fascism: the terror in the streets so characteristic of both Italy and Germany at that time.

The remainder of the play was, of necessity, drastically shortened. Even so, many observors were unaware to what extent. Heywood Broun of the *New Republic* (December 29, 1937) for one, realized that the play had indeed been cut but, surprisingly, insisted that "no changes have been made in the text." Grenville Vernon was another. In one *Commonweal* review (December 3, 1937) his only lament was that the production "leaves out what is to many the high moment of the tragedy, the appearance of Caesar's ghost." While admiring its energy, lively attack, sincerity, and bold theatrical intelligence, Stark Young was pretty much disappointed by the production; the actors clipped the form and glow of their lines, resulting for him in mere drabness. However, he was also quick to recognize that Welles, by hitting upon one of its fundamental themes, had made the original play relevant and accessible to present-day audiences.

Vernon, in his second *Commonweal* review (December 31, 1937), complained that in modernizing *Caesar* Welles had destroyed much of the poetry and music of the lines. However, when compared to the virtues of the production—its "sense of vitality," in particular—this was none too weighty an offense in Vernon's opinion, and he declared it "the most exciting presentation of the year."

But Welles, as always, had deliberately geared his production toward more popular sensibilities. With *Caesar*, as nowhere else, he was able to draw upon certain basic propositions (in this case, political) that the majority of his audience was not only in agreement with but eager to receive (such was liberal politics in New York City), and to give these propositions an archetypal immediacy by the strength of his theatrical acumen. He was sharing his convictions with them.

His level of awareness met, however, with less than unqualified enthusiasm from those of more thorough political grounding. *Current History* (April 1938) noted that *Julius Caesar* is no proletarian play, but was written, as were all Shakespeare's tragedies, in keeping with an aristocratic tradition.

No Welles production of Shakespeare ever received a unanimous reception or interpretation from the critics. And this is just what happened with *Julius Caesar*. John Mason Brown (*New York Post*, November 12, 1937) saw the play as a brilliant exposé of fascism; Joseph Wood Krutch (*The Nation*, November 27, 1937) saw it as the story of a conspiracy that went wrong because conspiracies are by nature corrupt and attract corrupt men to them; Grenville Vernon (*Commonweal*, December 2, 1937) saw it as neither fascist or anti-fascist because Shakespeare does not offer any exact parallels to modern events, although there are some strange likenesses; and Stark Young (*New Republic*, December 1, 1937) saw Brutus as glorifying the state. Yet all of them recognized it as one of the most absorbing productions to be seen in New York in many years. An interesting sidelight is that the *Daily Worker* review objected that the parallel was insufficient for an anti-fascist play, and to the "slanderous" picture of the masses being swayed by a demagogue.

Production by Orson Welles

From its inception the Mercury Theatre established the practice of placing the legend "Production by Orson Welles" directly beneath the title of the play and the name of its author. This credit was originated by his partner, John Houseman, who still maintains that it "means exactly what it says: they were Welles' shows."

There is little doubt that both the initial concepts of production and their eventual realization were largely of Welles's own doing. In this he is comparable to a director like Max Reinhardt. However, a Welles production never attained the totality that Gordon Craig dreamed of for the artist in the theatre, and among those with whom Welles had to collaborate were designers. His unwillingness to acknowledge their contributions often seemed so petty and willful as to cast a pall over his own, very real achievements.

Admittedly, there is a hazy line between a director's and a designer's role. Is the initial sketch (the germinal idea) the "design"? Or is it the carefully worked out presentation of that idea? Welles proceeded to make this a moot point by implying that he carried out the total design process to a far greater extent than in fact he had. It is, therefore, impossible to separate his actual contribution from what he was merely taking credit for under the blanket assurance that absolutely anything of importance in the production was, by definition, his alone to claim.

Welles got along beautifully with the members of the company who simply placed themselves into his hands (and there were many of them), and very badly with others, who, like Abe Feder, demanded their share in the rights of a temperamental genius. Welles's former wife, Virginia, likened the Mercury to a large family affair, with Welles (at age 22) as pater familias. If a family of actors was, in fact, Welles's ambition for the company, it went largely unrecognized. Most of them still remember it as a decidedly monolithic affair. Hiram Sherman, an early and steadfast disciple of Welles, has commented:

> How could you feel part of a collaborative effort when Orson took the credit for everything? You were supposed to surrender yourself, bask in his reflected glory and be satisfied.

If "Production by Orson Welles" had been meant as a statement of recognition due him as the Mercury's seminal and controlling intellect, it would have been a justifiable credit. Unfortunately, the effort was made to apply it to every detail of production. A similar dispute had arisen on *Dr. Faustus*, and, although the billing still read "Production by Orson Welles," Feder was given full credit for the lighting (despite Welles's claims that he had originated the effects).

Gabel's statement that "Orson designs everything he does himself," reflects a kind of mystique of the devotees, and relegated his designers to the position of mere draftsmen. Houseman admits that "some of the people around him [Welles] felt they were being used," while adding that for others "it was a wonderful collaborative experience."

Houseman was one of the builders of the mystique. An example of this is his statement in *Run-Through* that Welles returned from a ten-day retreat in New Hampshire with "a completely reedited text of *Julius Caesar* which included not only music and light cues," but also the "sketches and a plasticine model of his production." His statement then continues with the claim that Sam Leve "absorbed Orson's ideas and sketches. . .and under her [Jean Rosenthal's] technical direction set about converting them into working drawings and blueprints."[4] All of this is completely at variance with the recollection of Sam Leve, who was eventually credited with designing the performance.

By insisting that Welles had little to do with the design for *Julius Caesar* (or *The Shoemaker's Holiday*, for that matter), Leve must have seriously threatened that mystique — especially since his claim includes making both the original sketches and plasticine model, as well as upward of one hundred lighting effects, among them the famed Nuremburg lights.

Houseman and Leve likewise disagree about Rosenthal's part in all this. Leve maintains that she executed *his* lighting scheme and supervised the construction of the platforms in accordance with *his* specifications. (It may be noted that the platforms were found intact and the only construction necessary was to cut them down to size.) Welles directed the stagehands who put the set in place at the Mercury and, afterward, added an additional level to it. Leve sat at the light board with Welles for the readings and concedes that "Orson called the shots for that."

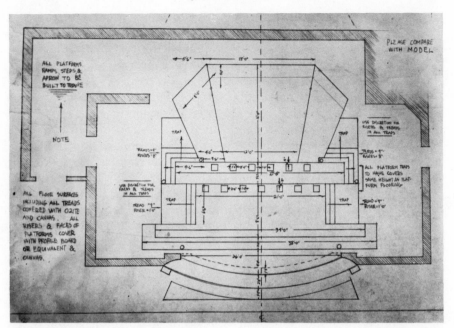

Samuel Leve's ground plan. . .

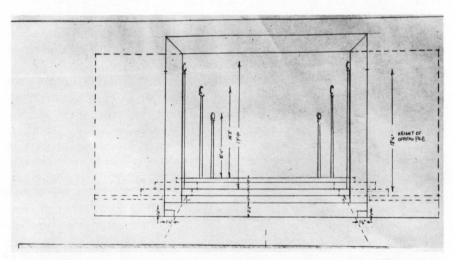

. . .and elevation for *Julius Caesar*. Only the downstage flagpoles, which were built into the stage facade, were used for the production. *Courtesy of Samuel Leve.*

Leve's ground plan illustrates a series of holes cut into the stage floor for the 500-watt up-lights (which were covered over with wire mesh). He has described how "smudge pots were located just offstage. The actors' natural movement carried the smoke on with them—and that's how the shaft [i.e., Nuremburg] effect was created." Both the ground plan and the elevation disclose a complicated arrangement of ramps, platforms, and traps that cover the Mercury stage in great detail. The two permanent flag poles are augmented in the drawings by a row each of four more moving upstage; however, these were omitted from the actual set. While the style and concept of the production is unquestionably Welles's, there is no reason to believe that these are not the work of Sam Leve and, accordingly, the creation and execution of the lights and setting.

Jean Rosenthal stated that when she raised the question of production credits, Houseman explained to her that "despite the incidental courtesies of the profession it was important that Orson be given sole credit for everything."[5] And indeed he was. On opening night Leve arrived at the theatre only to learn that his name had been omitted from the program.

By contrast to his insistence upon production credits, Welles, (with the exception of *Macbeth*) was unwilling to take any credit for the extensive reordering he did on most of his scripts. It may be that he felt that Shakespeare, Marlowe, and the others would be more acceptable to his audience without any coauthorship.

Despite the careful planning that had gone into the production, it was, from all accounts, a struggle to see it through. Much of this is attributable to Welles's lack of organization. "When he didn't want to rehearse a scene which he knew was wrong (like the Cinna the Poet Scene), he'd make up endless excuses not to." Fortunately, Welles was not restricted by any union regulations and, therefore, could (and did) rehearse whenever he preferred, which was generally in the middle of the night, when the city was quiet and there was nothing in the air to offend his concentration and artistic temperament.

Despite the brilliance of Welle's conception, when it came to the physical mounting of the production things got to be chaotic. While Welles was out front directing, he would have a stand-in on stage. But when it came time for him to be on stage, he was not likely to be anywhere near where his stand-in had been. This gave the show a sense of improvisation, which was not something the cast relished. Yet a sense of improvisation—or, if you will, a trial and error process—was bound up in all of his work.

Welles had dazzling ideas, but sometimes they occurred at the very last minute and left his actors feeling uneasy in their roles. A new ending was tried out every night for *Julius Caesar*—right up to the opening. As a result there was never an opportunity to rehearse the play from start to finish.

On the other hand, particular attention was paid to the crowd scenes, which were by no means as spontaneous as they appeared. As Hiram Sherman remembered:

We [the cast] spent endless hours doing nothing but ad-libs for the funeral scene. We all had to write out specific lines. You'd say three, four, nine words out of your speech; then somebody would stop you. And it worked, too, much better than in the twosome scenes.

By and large the acting was quite well received. Grenville Vernon thought it responsible for "the force and poignancy of the production." John Anderson called the acting "the complete expression of the idea. It's simple, easy, almost colloquial." Brook Atkinson commented: "For the most part the actors underplay it. . .He [George Coulouris] dominates the mob with sound in the one passage of declamatory eloquence in the performance." And for John Mason Brown, Joseph Holland's portrayal of Caesar was "alive and real enough to explain all Brutus' misgivings."

A most noticeably unorthodox piece of casting was that of Martin Gabel as a not-so-lean-and-hungry Cassius. "I had everything for the part," Gabel admitted, "except that I was physically wrong for it. Caesar comes on and says 'Yon Cassius has a lean and hungry look!' And there I stood, four-square, looking like a block of granite. I was once described by Walter Kerr as being 'built like an ice box.' " Welles may have meant this as more of a whimsical than an unorthodox note. At age 13 he, himself, had appeared as a not-so-lean-and-hungry Cassius in a Todd School production of *Caesar*, later doubling as Antony for the funeral oration.

It has been said of Welles that his own tendency as an actor was toward the melodramatic, even when underplaying a role. As Brutus, however, he is remembered by Joseph Cotton as "very straight and restrained. No bombast. But, then, it wasn't that kind of part." Somewhere during the run of the show he evidently lost interest in it, became bored, and at one point stopped trying. When the audience shouted, "Louder," Welles responded by simply glaring at them.

Many of the bit players and supernumeries were hangers-on. Apparently anyone who was in the theater might be called upon. Thus, James Morcum, whom Welles had brought in to design his forthcoming productions of *Too Much Johnson* and *Five Kings*, was pressed into service as an extra in *Caesar* (for one dollar a performance).

The program, while omitting any mention of the designer, listed "Music by Marc Blitzstein" directly below Welles's own credit. In an article for *Modern Music* (January-February 1938) Blitzstein stated:

The Fascist March which opens. . .*Julius Caesar* is. . .less an overture

Welles as Brutus standing over the Nuremberg lights. *Courtesy of Walter Ash.*

than an initial statement of theme, I had it cut off abruptly at
Caesar's first words "Bid every noise be still!" and one thinks immediately
back to it as the theatrical pivot up to that point.

In the same issue of *Modern Music* Aaron Copland applauded
Blitzstein's work, noting that "ten bars too many and a drama might
degenerate into melodrama. Marc Blitzstein saluted this truth last season
in *Julius Caesar*." Virgil Thomson, in the March-April 1938 issue, praised
the Mercury Theatre for "its sagacity in ordering incidental music from
Blitzstein for *Caesar*." (A caveat is needed in evaluating this criticism.
Blitzstein, Thomson, and Copland were, respectively, the two vice-
presidents and treasurer of the Arrow Music Press — a venture founded by
Lehman Engel.)

The best comment upon the production is the statement by Martin
Gabel describing the state of mind of the cast as opening night approached
— and the reception the play received.

All of us but Coulouris were very hopeful, but not really sanguine
until John Mason Brown came to that preview and was ecstatic
about it. Orson and Jack told us how much he'd liked it. Coulouris
suspected they were just psychologizing us so we'd be up for opening
night. But it turned out to be true. Opening night dowagers were
throwing their tiaras into the air. It was a very great evening in the
theatre.

7

The Shoemaker's Holiday

In a sense *The Shoemaker's Holiday* was, like *Julius Caesar*, a propaganda piece. Welles's comic imagery was every bit as compelling and immediate as his images of disaster had been; this time, however, they closely paralleled the happiest notions of American domesticity. The values common to all sentimental comedy (the triumph of loving hearts, the kindly boss who prospers, the nobility of the working class) abounded in *Shoemaker*. Welles turned the apparent distance between the play's original milieu and his own day into a license for depicting the contemporary world in the earthiest possible terms. The audience's laughter was solicited on the level of contemporary attitudes toward sexuality — attitudes that had earlier made burlesque and so-called naughty language so much a part of the popular culture.

Welles, in editing the text, began by reducing it to its sentimental framework and, upon this, built his production. He looked upon *Shoemaker* as a domestic drama, reflecting the life of the Shakespearean period. He compared it with *The First Year*, a play running on Broadway in the late 1930s. He thought that a half-century later *The First Year* would similarly be considered a reflection of American life in the 1930s. Of course, he was wrong on both counts.

Shoemaker was no more a vision of the Elizabethans than *The First Year* was of life during the thirties. Both were illusory images; but *Shoemaker*, at least, was an accurate reflection of what people laughed at, what they found satisfying — and, above all, what they really wished life were like.

Brooks Atkinson (in the *New York Times*, January 3, 1938) described the production as "an uproarious comic strip of Elizabethan fooling," and, indeed, Welles's intentions were precisely that. Acknowledging that his characters were not *real* people (in the sense of psychological drama), he infused them with all the vivid two-dimensional simplicity that one associates with caricatures.

In brief scenes with truncated dialogue, he reduced the complexities of the plot to a point where each scene "told" its joke and was over. The "joke" was generally sexual. Specifically, it was a juvenile sexuality. As Hiram Sherman described it, "All the groupings and firkings were like children's horseplay. We were children saying dirty words."

Welles shied away from the emotional committment that real sexuality implies. Blue humor has, of course, its deeper side. But, by keeping it on the relatively harmless level of off-color stories, Welles titilated his audience without disturbing them.

Shoemaker managed to maintain a certain overall tension by appearing to be on the verge of saying more than was intended. He did so by stressing possible double-meanings for seemingly innocuous antics, foremost among which was his use of eminently acceptable words in such a way that their emotive value far outweighed any apparent meaning. The most obvious example of this was the word *firk*, which actually means "to frisk." However, *firk* sounds enough like *fuck* to serve as *fuck*, and, reinforced by various sight-gags, that is exactly how the Mercury audience understood it. Other four-letter words, such as *fart*, were also utilized for the maximum intensity of the reaction they could provoke. Welles relied on their total expressive value, rather than on the actual dialogue itself. Reading his script today, one is hard pressed to locate these "dirty words"; indeed, it seems almost pristine in its cleanliness.

By retelling Dekker's conventional story through a series of immediate and calculated responses to his audience's sensibilities, Welles was able, as described in *Stage* (February 1938), to present "a lusty May-Day hymn to the joys of procreation; a Bronx cheer for fashionable homosexuality." To be sure, there is barely a hint of procreation and nothing about homosexuality in the script. Yet the production was, in fact, about sex and its assorted delights, as much as *Caesar* was about social upheaval and all its horrors.

The Shoemaker's Holiday opened at the Mercury Theatre on January 1, 1938, and was instantly hailed by Brooks Atkinson of the *New York Times*: "the funniest jig of the season and the New Year has begun with a burst of theatrical hilarity." Audiences, in responding to *Julius Caesar*, had seen their worst fears given understandable, if terrifying, form. *Shoemaker*, in its wish fulfilling way, caught their mood just as intuitively.

The set was designed with the tempo of the show clearly in mind. Despite the debate over who was actually responsible for the design, the production relied most heavily on a feature that Welles is said, by all accounts, to have insisted upon. Three curtains were placed at logical intervals across the stage. Their pulling separated the scenes and accelerated the production's overall pace. To a number of critics, George

Jean Nathan (*Newsweek*, January 17, 1938) among them, the sheer brevity of the evening was a virtue for its own sake.

> Let us, in the name of intelligence and satisfying entertainment, have more of these one hour or one hour and a half plays. The two and one half hours regularly, arbitrarily, and foolishly imposed upon us have done much to hurt the theatre.

Notable among the few dissenters was John Gassner. Writing in *One Act Play Magazine* (January 1938), he said that "as a play, *The Shoemaker's Holiday* is so creaky that even the direction tacitly admits as much. . . . The staging devices are, after all, fairly obvious; and although the burlesque spirit of the production gives the play a little life on the stage, it. . .is as a series of glittering fragments stuck in a matrix of obvious horseplay."

View of *The Shoemaker's Holiday* from backstage of one of the rows of houses. *Courtesy of Hiram Sherman.*

Many critics realized that an essential part of the humor was the effect of the "dirty" language. A number of them were willing (as, undoubtedly, Welles had hoped) to attach such language to the nature of the play rather than to his production. Even Gassner was thus fooled. For him, Welles had not "pussyfooted in the matter of obscenity, which is in this case an understandable reflection of a robust environment and an exuberant spirit."

In this matter of language, Welles is credited with breaking new ground for Broadway. Sidney Whipple of the *New York World Telegram* (January 3, 1938) noted that "it must have required boldness to defy the grundyism that inevitably would be shocked at the robust figures of speech which Dekker (in common with his compeer, Shakespeare) used with honest abandon."

George Jean Nathan, who appreciated Welles's pioneering spirit, applauded the fact that "the only two remaining four-letter words not yet spoken from the American stage duly receive their belated hearing." He went on to scoff at the damage such language was likely to have upon "the sensibilities of the contemporary polloi." Burns Mantle of the *Daily News* (January 3, 1938), who was generally offended by the production, commented wryly, "All the words are there, and so, too, are the costuming vulgarities."

Although Welles reduced the text to the bare framework of a sentimental love story, he still managed to retain most of Dekker's plot line, with the few structural revisions (Rose recognizes Lacy and Simon becomes Lord Mayor earlier in his text) serving to speed matters along. Welles himself described it as the story of Simon Eyre, a shoemaker who rises in the world, of his wife who enjoys her rise in society, and of the people who surround them.

But neither the Horatio Alger-like story of Simon's prosperity nor the matings and partings of the lovers were what visitors to the Mercury took such pleasure in. For most of them, *Shoemaker* was chiefly the prank of a group of roguish and bawdy apprentices who sang over their stitching and cavorted through the streets of London.

The Shoemaker's Holiday depicts "experience" with the same sensibilities as its leading character, Firk, the embodiment of a kind of benign animality. It would be overstating the case to say that the production was seen through his eyes; yet it is Firk who becomes the "norm," while the serious bourgeois morality of the lovers finally emerges as an absence of feeling.

Welles played the workmen's plot against the love story as two contrasting states of feeling, the one reflecting upon the other. The "unnatural" love story was not intended to move the audience directly, but, rather, to make the "natural" feelings of the workmen more vivid. *Shoemaker* was by no means a direct attack on bourgeois customs and morality. However, the essential mood of the play was that of the earthy and the unrestrained triumphing over the civilized and the controlled — and in such a way as to make it appear both morally and emotionally superior. Welles invited one and all to bask in the pleasures of free and illicit behavior. Indeed, the play's highly conventional ending only served to confirm the viability of the "forbidden." The audience's intense delight was that an experience that had heretofore been thought of as sordid had become acceptable and enlightened.

Scenes, such as the workmen's revolt, were explicit not only within the production's expressive framework, but also within the context of the play's contemporary meaning as well. The following from Dekker's second act is an example of how Welles edited Dekker and made him appear so contemporary.

Welles' version (unpublished)
(Enter LACY, as HANS, singing)

HODGE
Master, here comes some outlandish workman.

FIRK
Hire him, good master, that I might learn some gibble-gabble.

EYRE
No, no, Firk. Let him vanish. We have journeymen enough.

HANS
He was also dronck he cold myet stand, Upsoloe sie byen.

HODGE & FIRK
Upsoloe sid byen.

HODGE
T'will make us work the faster.

MARGERY
God's me we have not men enough, but we must entertain every butter-box.

Dekker version (Modern Library)
(Enter Lacy, disguised as Hans, singing)

FIRK
Master, for my life, yonder's a brother of the Gentle Craft; if he bear not Saint Hugh's bones, I'll forfeit my bones; he's some uplandish workman: hire him, good master, that I may learn some gibble-gabble; 'twill make us work the faster.

EYRE
Peace, Firk! A hard world! Let him pass; let him vanish; we have journeymen enow. Peace, my fine Firk!

MARGERY
May, may y' are best follow your man's counsel; you shall see what will come on't; we have not man enow, but we must entertain every butter-box; but let that pass.

HODGE

Fore God a proper man?

FIRK

And I warrant a fine workman.

BOY

Hire him, Master/

EYRE

No, no, we have journey-men enough.

HODGE

Master farewell; dame, adieu; if such a man as he cannot find work, Hodge is not for you.

EYRE

Nay, tarry Hodge.

FIRK

If Roger remove, Firk follows.

EYRE

You arms of my trade you pillars of my profession.

HODGE

Fare ye well, master.

MARGERY

Nay, let them go.

FIRK

Goodbye dame.

MARGERY

There be more men than Hodge and more fools than Firk.

FIRK

Fools?

HODGE

Dame, 'fore God, if my master follow your counsel, he'll consume little beef. He shall be glad of men, and he can catch them.

FIRK

Ay, that he shall.

HODGE

'Fore God, a proper man, and I warrant, a fine workman. Master, farewell; dame, adieu; if such a man as he cannot find work, Hodge is not for you.

EYRE

Stay, my fine Hodge.

FIRK

Faith, an your foreman go, dame, you must take a journey to seek a new journeyman; if Roger remove, Firk follows. If Saint Hugh's bones shall not be set a-work, I may prick mine awl in the walls, and go play. Fare ye well, master; goodpbye dame.

EYRE

Tarry, my fine Hodge, my brisk foreman! Stay, Firk! — Peace, pudding-broth! By the Lord of Ludgate, I love my men as my life. Peace, you gallimafry! Hodge, if he want work, I'll hire him. One of you to him; stay — he comes to us.

LACY

Goeden dach, meester, ende u vro oak.

EYRE

Peace, you barley pudding
full of maggots, quarrel
not with me and my men.

HODGE

Here's an inventory of
my shop tools.

EYRE

Nay, stay, Hodge. By
this beard she shall not
meddle with thee. Have
I not ta'en you from
selling tripes in Eastcheap,
And set you in my shop and
made you hail-fellow with
Simon Eyre The Shoemaker?
In, you queen of clubs.
If he want work, I'll hire
him. Good day friend.

(Exit Marg.)

LACY

Goeden dach, maester, ende u
vro oak.

EYRE

Well, friend, oak, are you
of the gentle craft?

LACY

Yaw, yaw, ik ben den skaw-
maker.

HODGE

Hark you skawmakers have
you all your tools?

FIRK

A good rubbin pin, a good
stopper, your four sorts of
awls, and your two balls —

LACY

Yaw, yaw.

FIRK

Nails, if I should speak after
him without drinking, I should
choke. And you, friend Oake,
are you of the Gentle Craft?

LACY

Yaw, yaw, ik bin den skomawker.

FIRK

Den skomaker, quoth a!
And hark you, skomaker, have
you all your tools, a good
rubbing-pin, a good stopper,
a good dresser, your four
sorts of awls, and your two
balls of wax, your paring
knife, your hand- and thumb-
leathers, and good St. Hugh's
bones to smooth up your work?

LACY

Yaw, yaw; be niet vorveard.
Ik hab all de dingen voour
mack skooes groot and cleane.

FIRK

Ha, ha! Good master, hire
him; he'll make me laugh so
that I shall work more in
mirth than I can in earnest.

EYRE

Hear ye, friend, have ye any
skill in the myster of

EYRE

Hear ye, friend, have ye any
skill in the mystery of
cordwainers?

LACY

Ik weet niet wat yow seg? ich
verstaw you niet.

HODGE

of wax.

LACY

Ik hab all de dingen.

EYRE

What is thy name?

LACY

Hans — ? Hans.

EYRE

Give me thy hand, Hans.
Thou art welcome. Boy, bid
the tapster of the boar's
head fill me a dozen cans of
beer for my journey-man.

FIRK

A dozen cans? Oh, Hodge,
now I'll stay.

EYRE

A DOZEN cans of beer, I
tell you, and he that fills
any more than two pays for
them.

(Enter Margery)

MARGERY

Simon, it is almost seven!

EYRE

Is't so, Dame Clapper,
dungeon? Almost seven o'-
clock and my men's break-
fast not ready yet! Rip you
brown bread tanken (exit
Marg.) Come Hans, come my
men. To work awhile, and then
to breakfast.

(Exit Eyre)

LACY

Yaw, yaw, yaw.

FIRK

Why, thus, man: (Imitating by
gesture a shoemaker at work).
Ich verste u niet, quoth a.

LACY

Yaw, yaw, yaw; ick can dat
wel doen.

FIRK

Yaw yaw! He speaks yawing like
a jackdaw that gapes to be
fed with cheese-curds. Oh,
he'll give a villainous pull
at a can of double-beer; but
Hodge and I have the vantage,
we must drink first, because
we are the eldest journeymen.

EYRE

Why is thy name?

HANS

Hans — Hans Meulter.

EYRE

Give me thy hand; th' art
welcome. — Hodge, entertain
him; Firk, bid him wel-
come; come, Hans. Run,
wife, bid your maids, your
trullibuds, make ready my
fine men's breakfasts. To
him, Hodge!

HODGE

Hans, th' art welcome; use
thyself friendly, for we are
good fellows; if not, thou
shalt be fought with, wert
thou bigger than a giant.

FIRK

Yea, and drunk with, wert
thou Gargantua. My master
keeps no cowards, I tell
thee. — Ho, boy, bring him
an heel-block, here's a new
journeyman.

FIRK

Yaw, yaw! Oh, he'll give a
villainous pull at a double
can of beer.

(Enter boy with beer)

HODGE

This beer came hopping in
quickly.

FIRK

Yes, Hodge, we must drink
first, because we are the
eldest yourneymen.

(Hodge takes Firk's
beer and exits. . .)

Alack, alack
Girls hold out tack
For now smocks of this
    jumbling
Shall go to wrack.

(Firk is interrupted
by Hammon singing.
Firk exits.)

(Enter Boy)

LACY

O, ich wersto you; ich moet
een halve dossen cans
betaelen; here, boy, nempt
dis skilling, tap eens
freelicke.

(Exit Boy)

EYRE

Quick, snipper-snapper, away!
Firk, scour thy throat, thou
shalt wash it with Castilian
liquor.

(Enter Boy)

Come, my last of the fives,
give me a can. Have to
thee, Hans; here, Hodge; here,
Firk; drink, you mad Greeks,
and work like tru Trojans,
and pray for Simon Eyre, the
shoemaker. — Here, Hans, and
th'art welcome.

FIRK

Lo, dame, you would have
lost a good fellow that
will teach us to laugh.
This beer came hopping in
well.

MARGERY

Simon, it is almost seven.

EYRE

Is't so, Dame Clapper-
dudgeon? Is't seven a
clock, and my men's breakfast not ready? Trip and
go, you soused conger,
away! Come, you mad
hyperboreans; follow me,
Hodge; follow me, Hans; come
after, my fine Firk; to

work, to work a while, and
then to breakfast!

(Exit)

FIRK

Soft! Yaw, yaw, good Hans,
though my master have no
more wit but to call you
afore me, I am not so
foolish to go behind you, I
being the elder journeyman.

(Exeunt)

In no way did the Mercury production violate Dekker's narrative
line. However, in *Shoemaker*, as in *Caesar*, Welles's concept of the play
was wholly in accordance with the dictates of popular culture. The
production's appeal was largely emotional. But that did not prevent its
also being understood in contemporary sociopolitical terms.

The workmen's scenes were of particular interest to critics who enjoyed
drawing political parallels. John Mason Brown of the *New York Post*
(January 3, 1938) was much impressed: "The common people are the
subject of Dekker's comedy. They hold their heads high, even if their
minds are not always elevated. . . .Yet they are free men who are willing
to strike at a moment's notice in the interest of an abused fellow crafts-
man." John Gassner, however, was unimpressed by the play's political
significance. He thought it dated and its egalitarianism like a high school
exercise. However, *Stage* (February 1938) found that *The Shoemaker's
Holiday* was, indeed, a glimpse at "the source-stream of British democracy,
the Mother Goose days of trade unionism."

In responding to the play's treatment of the everyday lives of the
common people, the Mercury audience was responding to the popular
myths surrounding the origins of democracy rather than the social and
economic causes that not only made democracy possible but inevitable.

For all their pretensions to egalitarianism, the Mercury audience
was primarily an elitist group. They were the liberal champions of the
workingman, but not "workers" themselves. However, while they might
more readily identify with Sir Rowland Lacy than with Firk, the audience
still longed to feel themselves at one with the common man. Welles's
production made it possible for them to do this painlessly. They could
experience a vicarious enjoyment from behavior that spurned the morals
and ethical standards most of them observed outside the theatre. And it

was this extreme contrast between conventional attitudes and the essential experience that distinguished Welles's production of *The Shoemaker's Holiday* from the other sentimental comedies of its day.

The set for *Shoemaker*, with its natural textures in place of colors and realistic details, created an imaginary and enclosed world, which was itself in contrast to the earthy appeal of the production. "Once again," Houseman tells us, "the set design was Orson's, executed by Samuel Leve under Jean Rosenthal's supervision."[1] Leve maintains, as he does with *Julius Caesar*, that the design for *Shoemaker* was his alone.

This use of textures to connote common social strata was just what Welles wanted. The *Shoemaker* set was an abstract rendering of an Elizabethan village. On either side of the stage there was a row of three

From left to right—Marian Warring-Manley as Margery, Whitford Kane as Simon Eyre, and George Coulouris as the King. *Courtesy of Hiram Sherman.*

houses, and in front of each of these, a small enclosed area. Draw curtains hung across those two areas, and a third across the center.

Shoemaker played in repertory with *Julius Caesar*, and, for the former *Caesar's* blood-red well was covered with a burlap cyclorama. This provided the neutral background that the production required, as well as adding to its sense of enclosure. By its lack of detail, the set was able to convey the impression of the Elizabethan period without also being tied to its specific realities.

The arrangement of the ramps used for *Caesar* was reversed, so that they started at what would normally be the footlights and rose to the rear of the stage. Entrances were made between the playing areas downstage and the houses, which were separated by two foot passageways. The houses themselves were made of natural pine slats without either doors or windows.

Unlike the set, Millia Davenport's costumes were highly realistic. She apparently was given a free hand in their design, except for Welles's idea (which she said delighted her) that they use codpieces. "The first time in the American theatre! It was marvellous!" The actors found their costumes an endless source of stage business. According to Davenport, this was particularly true of Hiram Sherman:

Chubby was the slob in *Shoemaker*. He had the most revolting triangle of shoe leather—absolutely unmanageable—tied on with thongs, which kept coming undone. And he spent his entire time on-stage keeping himself decent. It was the most adorable thing anyone has ever seen.

To which Sherman replied: "I played with my codpiece because usually my salary was stashed in it. It was to protect my gross."

This kind of raw, rather naive pleasure was typical of the production's immediate appeal. "It was bawdy for its time," Norman Lloyd remembers. "The codpieces were enlarged beyond all human proportions."

More than any of Welles's other productions *The Shoemaker's Holiday* depended heavily on the performances of his actors, particularly their sense of timing. He was, as John Mason Brown (*New York Post*, January 3, 1938) duly noted in his review of the show, able to attract an "increasingly impressive list of actors who, with reason and the theatre's best interests at heart, have rallied under his conquering banner." The most important of these was Hiram Sherman, whose racy humanity was clearly the catalyst of the production. The humor in *Shoemaker* was not only of a kind that Welles thought his audience would respond to, but the kind that he personally revelled in.

The same spirit of fun that so dominated the production was also reflected in rehearsals. To Norman Lloyd, who played Hodge, "Welles was not much of a disciplinarian. A madman, yes—but no disciplinarian."

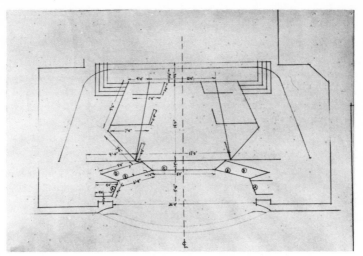

Leve's ground plan and. . .

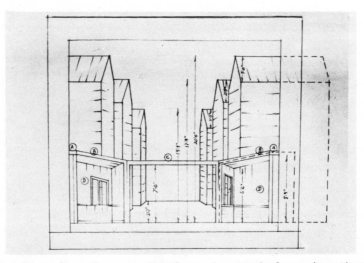

. . .elevation for the production. Legend for elevation: All dimensions are given from STAGE floor. All construction must be plumb. Build bases of houses to stand firmly on all platform heights. Stage braces will support houses. A—old fashioned vaudeville entrances but bear no curtains. Follow same construction as B and C, but have no track on rear. B—beam bearing curtain 50% fullness on single track. C—beam bearing curtain 50% fullness on double track, having one foot overlap on center. D—removable units with flooring riding on domes. Dimensions on roofs given in height, the hypotenuse or the slope to be determined. *Courtesy of Samuel Leve.*

Evidently Lloyd and Joseph Cotton (Rowland Lacy) were able to do pretty nearly what they pleased. "Welles held a loose rein on *Shoemaker*. He'd just laugh and say 'a little more upstage!' "

Other members of the production had a different impression. Composer Lehman Engel was not swept up in the general hilarity, and drew a sharp distinction between the atmosphere of the finished production and that of rehearsals.

> Everything was mechanical in that he [Welles] used the actors exactly like robots. He'd say "alright Joe [Cotton], on the count of three the curtain slides back [and the curtain did indeed do just that] and you'll appear and stand one, two. . . .Walk, four, five, six, seven, eight, nine, ten. Turn twelve, thirteen, fourteen, fifteen, sixteen. STOP!!!!!" He might laugh at something, and then have an actor do a piece of business he'd devise ten times until the actor knew it mechanically. He never bothered to explain a characterization, never in my hearing anyway. He'd say how he wanted it and direct every single thing: "Start off on your right foot, and when you get to that chair, turn around. No, no—upstage. Then sit. Now, I want your right foot straight out and your left foot just behind it." He moulded you. Orson only knew his own way and that was "Now, everybody keep quiet and I'll tell you what to do." That was his only way of working. He simply didn't know any other.[2]

A lot of Firk's business was thought up by the actor himself, aided and abetted by Welles.

> Chubby would do something and Welles would double over with laughter, saying "good—now do this!" It was a kind of partnership between director and actor.

While not exactly overjoyed with his role in this "partnership," Sherman was certainly satisfied with the way it showed him off. John Mason Brown said in his review that "Hiram Sherman as Firk gives by all odds the finest, the funniest interpretation of an Elizabethan low comedy character we have ever seen." Looking back on the experience, however, Sherman had this to say:

> Welles was a choreographer. You'd turn here and go around there. This is where he and I fall out. I don't believe you can choreograph a comic routine and make it comic in terms of movement alone—especially, if there is nothing funny about it to begin with. We had a lot of "You go around in back of Norman. Norman goes back of you." Being spaced around. Having to hold a position endlessly. You get cramps that way, not laughs.

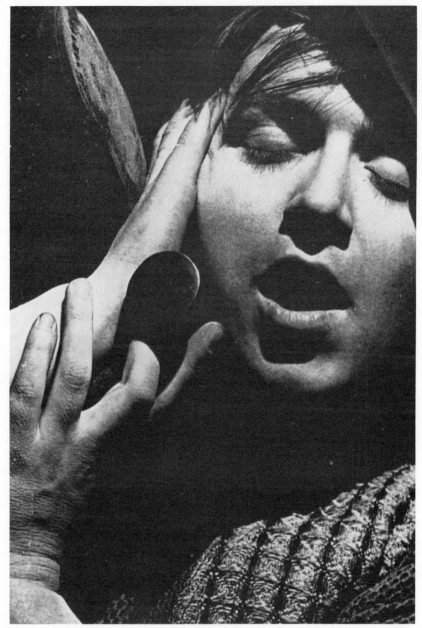

Hiram Sherman as Firk, fondling a shoe. *Courtesy of Hiram Sherman.*

Firk was the focal point of the play, and a running gag that developed during rehearsals greatly enhanced his importance in the production. Arthur Anderson, who appeared as the Boy, described it:

This was one of those accidents. Orson didn't think it up, but to his credit, when it happened, he had the good sense to leave it in. Firk was supposed to go through a draw-curtain, ostensibly into the house beyond. But there was a miscue and just as he came to the curtain, it closed in his face. Zip—like that! So, he turned to the audience and did a kind of Stan Laurel reaction. It showed the frustration of a man who wants very much to do something but is denied by fate. That's always a good laugh. So, Chubby and Welles worked it up into a running gag. Everytime Firk tried to go through one of those curtains, it would close on him. They pursued it right to the end of the show. Chubby was about to make a closing speech and the house curtain came down on that, too.

Another convention that Welles employed in *Shoemaker* was the over-lapping of dialogue.

He loved you to bite the cue. Everything had to mesh, go together. You didn't finish a speech that someone else wasn't on top of you—all the time. This kind of repartee was very effective in *Shoemaker*. It was going lickity-split all the time. There was no wasted time at all. We didn't even have an interval. We did for one preview, but Orson decided to cut that and plow on without it.

Despite his objections to being precision engineered, Sherman was quick to realize that Welles had reordered the play into a vehicle for him.

The way our script was arranged I seemed to be the catalyst. Firk was promoted to the one who was always going up to the quality and insulting them, or talking back to his master. Orson built up my part so that I'd end a scene. Rather than my having a thing in the middle, he made a curtain out of it. It was all very flattering to me.

The Shoemaker's Holiday proved to be an enormously successful follow-up to *Julius Caesar*. In the space of just seven weeks and two productions, the Mercury Theatre had become, as described by Richard Watts of the *Herald Tribune* (January 3, 1938), "the great comfort of the theatrical season." Welles himself was called by John Mason Brown "one of the white hopes of our stage."

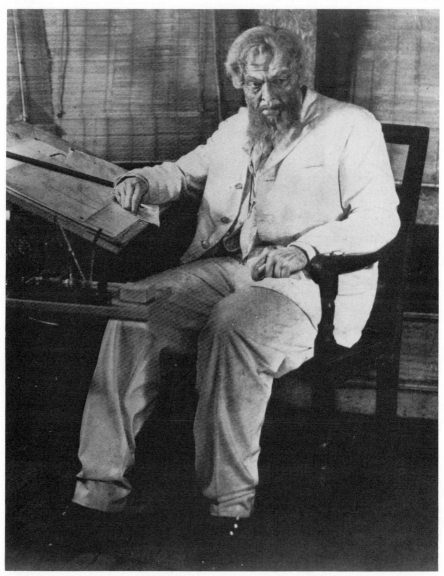

Welles as Captain Shotover in his own Mercury production of *Heartbreak House* (April 29, 1937). *Courtesy of Hortense and Roger Hill.*

Welles, in the full flush of his success, returns to visit the Todd School for Boys in 1938. His former headmaster and lifelong mentor, Roger Hill, is to his immediate left. *Courtesy of Hortense and Roger Hill.*

8

Danton's Death

The Mercury Theatre had concluded the 1937-38 season with its plans for the future still very much up in the air. On the strength of Hiram Sherman's personal notices as the rowdy but endearing apprentice, Firk, in *The Shoemaker's Holiday*, Welles cast about for another vehicle that would show off his versatile friend. He chose *The Importance of Being Earnest*, reordered around Sherman as Algernon Moncrieff. But more to the point, Welles and Houseman felt that *Earnest*, if run in repertory with *Shoemaker,* would not only have maintained the Mercury's identity but would keep it profitable and in the public favor while they could concentrate on the serious work for the season — *Five Kings.*

No sooner had they announced these plans than they had to scrap them as the result of (as Houseman put it) Sherman's sudden and "malignant treachery" — that is to say, his defection to the commercial theatre. Houseman insists that Sherman was fully aware of their plans, to which Sherman, with equal insistence, has responded, "Orson never so much as mentioned wanting me in anything after *Shoemaker*." Both Houseman and Sherman are supported in their positions by other members of the company.

Houseman's further charge — that Sherman's leaving caused the Mercury's change of fortune — seems unfair, to say the least. In addition to Sherman, the company lost such mainstays as Norman Lloyd, Whitford Kane, and George Coulouris between seasons — and Vincent Price, who, like Sherman, figured prominently in the decision to run *Earnest* and *Shoemaker* in repertory.

Foremost in the Welles-Houseman planning was the tremendous impact that *Julius Caesar* had made on critics and audiences alike. They thought that somehow the coming season had to be gotten underway at least as impressively. Strategy meetings were held, out of which came the decision to replace *Earnest* and *Shoemaker* with two entirely different plays, *Too Much Johnson* and *Danton's Death* — and to open them one night after the other. Both plays had already been on the Mercury's list of possibilities. Although *Johnson* was not Houseman's favorite piece, Welles assured him that, with a new production idea he had in mind, it would be funnier than *Horse Eats Hat*.

The Plan was to try out *Too Much Johnson* at a small summer theater operated by two of the Mercury apprentices at Stony Creek, Connecticut, where it could be shown to an audience with only a minimum of expense. Welles's production idea involved the integration of live and filmed sequences. Unfortunately, projection facilities were not available at Stony Creek. But the great problem with this production was financing, and the budget for fully realizing it was simply more than the Mercury could raise. The film sequences, while all shot, were never edited. Indeed, Houseman and Welles were so far in arrears with the laboratories that much of the footage was never released to them. Every trace of this film has since been lost.

Too Much Johnson was never performed in its entirety at Stony Creek. The production did receive considerable local attention, and try-outs were extended for a second week. John Houseman, more discerning than Welles, found it tedious and underrehearsed. He was opposed to its being offered as the opening production of the Mercury Theatre's second season. When it became obvious that *Too Much Johnson* would involve considerable expense, the production was shelved.

Just as the lack of money had been the deciding factor in the aborting of *Too Much Johnson*, so the expectation of funds has been said to be the deciding factor in the selection of *Danton's Death* as the next production. Houseman states that the decision was made one afternoon when Martin Gabel came into a radio rehearsal, threw the text of *Danton* on a table, and suggested that the company do it. It has been offered that Gabel wanted to use the production as a starring vehicle for himself as Danton and that he was its major contributor.

Houseman tells us that Welles had a number of difficulties with *Danton's Death*, using such words as "unprepared" and "uncertain" to describe the situation. The first difficulty, according to Houseman, was that Büchner's original text lacked the structure (that Welles had found in Shakespeare's *Julius Caesar*) and texture (that he had found in Marlowe's *Dr. Faustus*) around which Welles could develop his improvisations and variations. Another factor was the great success of Max Reinhardt's production some ten years earlier. Since Reinhardt's production had been a mass spectacle, Welles was going to make of his a drama of the individual and the mob, keeping the mob ever present, but rarely visible.

Welles may indeed have approached *Danton's Death* "unprepared and uncertain," but it was not for lack of a concept. The fact is that it had been Welles, and not Shakespeare and Marlowe, who supplied both the texture and structure for his productions of *Caesar* and *Dr. Faustus*.

Houseman suggests that what Welles had in mind was a production

Welles directing Joseph Cotton in one of the filmed sequences for *Too Much Johnson*. The scene, supposedly set in Cuba, was shot at a rock quarry in Haverstraw, New York. A Yonkers theater operated by Mercury stage manager Walter Ash was used to film the interiors. *Courtesy of Walter Ash.*

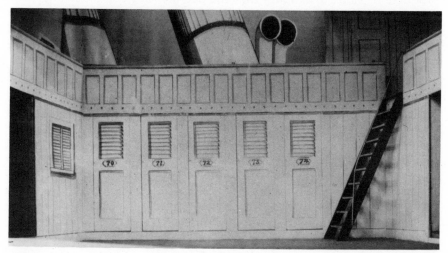

James Morcom's setting for act 1 of *Too Much Johnson* at the Stony Creek Summer Theater. Welles's "new production idea" included a filmed prologue of a chase around New York with everyone ending up aboard ship, which was to be on the stage. *Courtesy of James Morcom.*

Welles, wife Virginia in his lap, and other members of the cast for *Too Much Johnson* enjoying a rehearsal break outside their Connecticut theater. *Courtesy of Virginia Pringle.*

meant to please a general audience. But that, too, was obviously not the case. Welles knew better than anyone the root sentiment that dominated members of his audience. They were, first and foremost, attracted to the notion of political solutions to social problems; and, if there were any doubts about this, they faced them uneasily. They were ready to display the proper response to such ills as dictatorships and revolutions, but in the theatre expected their fears and apprehensions to be clearly defined and, if possible, coped with. In precluding even the possibility of a conventionalized response to so highly charged an experience, *Danton's Death* violated the tenets of popular theatre. And high art proved to be a poor substitute.

Of all his productions *Danton's Death* is the closest to expressionist drama, and it can be regarded as a further development of his work in

Julius Caesar. In *Caesar*, however, the images were more closely tied to an objective reality; in *Danton* their impact was far more subjective. Welles's "message" in both plays was identical: life leads to disaster; we are surrounded by death and destruction. The very simplicity of the message, in rhetorical terms, confounded his audience. The cyclorama of skulls in *Danton* formed an enveloping image comparable to the blood-red wall in *Caesar*. In *Danton*, however, this image not only dominated the objective action but the inner life of the characters as well. The characters were perceived, not only through what they were saying, but also as the result of their saying it in the constant shadow of this abstract representation of death.

Welles showed the French Revolution through his subjective impression of it. Clearly and unmistakably the emotional response he hoped for was that the Revolution, like all wars, is an exercise in futility. Danton and Robespierre reflected two possible responses to life, with neither adequate to the task of coping with the chaos that surrounded them. The play's "message," therefore, became an unrelieved evocation of the absurdity of the human condition. Nor was the central concern of the production a working out of revolutionary problems; instead, with revolution as a backdrop, the essence of man was to be revealed. By simplifying the historical meaning of his characters, Welles did not falter in his understanding of revolution. The characters became universal, and the Revolution itself became a metaphor for a state of existence, rather than an important political manifestation.

Welles's original concept of a drama of the individual and the mob emerged finally as an attempt to oppose the private world of his characters to the political arena of the Revolution. However real and personal Danton's sufferings (and, for that matter, Robespierre's in his one brief soliloquy), they only serve to further illuminate a predominantly nihilistic world view. As the play unfolds, the Dantonists move away from any active involvements, on the one hand, and toward becoming the very embodiment of man caught in "the terrible fatalism of history," on the other. Even their most private anguish points to the meaninglessness of all life. Robespierre's obsession with perpetuating the revolution seems little more than a reassertion of the cycle of despair and destruction that already dominates every image of the play.

Ending the play with St. Just's speech before the Assembly (delivered by Welles directly to the audience) merely made things confusing. Since he had taken no position on St. Just, Welles may have assumed that by giving him the last word he would be reflecting a view that everyone could live with. Indeed, the speech achieves a level of exultation beyond the reach of Robespierre's pragmatic rote (i.e., know who your enemies are, the business of national security, etc.). However, St. Just's "idealism," while purporting to be about human progress—"The human race is going

Vladimir Sokoloff as Robespierre (*left*) and Martin Gabel as Danton (*right*) standing before the cyclorama of skulls. *Courtesy of Martin Gabel.*

to rise from the cauldron of blood, as the earth did once from the waters of sin, rise with mighty strength in its limbs!"—is actually a parody of the high-flown expressions about freedom and dignity that marked the climactic moment of so many classical German dramas. As such, it bears a close resemblance to Hitler's rhetoric, and, seen in such a light, under-scores Büchner's skepticism about the validity of rhetoric in voicing any human ideals.

Coming as it did, however, as a sort of afterthought, the speech had the effect of nullifying whatever attitude had been expressed by the rest of the play, and it did so without assuming a positive stance of its own.

The attempt to justify the revolution through St. Just's speech seems an arbitrary conclusion to a production whose nihilism was apparent from the rise of the curtain; indeed, had it not come across so directly, the production might not have been as forcefully rejected as it was.

Left to right—Welles as Saint-Just and Eustace Wyatt as Fouquier. *Courtesy of Hortense and Roger Hill.*

Despite his attempt to change the political emphasis, Welles's production became an expression of the psychological effects of revolution. Its dramatic statement had little to do with actual politics. Danton, Robespierre, and the others were tormented men who happened to be about the business of revolution. Had theirs been a less emotionally charged involvement, this same production, while it might not have been greeted with rousing enthusiasm, would, at any other point in time, certainly have been spared the hostilities it aroused.

Since any concept was bound to point up inescapable parallels to the Trotsky-Stalin schism, the obvious move for Welles was to align audience sympathies with Danton and to villainize Robespierre in the same melodramatic terms he had used so effectively in *Julius Caesar*. But doing so would have meant slanting the play even further against revolution. On the other hand, throwing the weight of argument in Robespierre's favor would only have served to make the bloody excesses of the Revolution equally repulsive.

Whatever its troubles, *Danton's Death* is remembered as one of Welles's most ambitious stage conceptions. In a sense, it was more complicated even than *Five Kings*. The back wall was curved from the basement to the grid (approximately sixty feet) and spotted with thousands of Halloween masks, looking like a congress of death's heads and symbolic of the mob. The set and/or stage (they were one and the same for this production) was built back up from the basement in the form of an elevator that served for all scenes, whether as a rostrum, as a room, or, in the final scene, as it rose slowly to its full height—as the guillotine.

Each scene had a different level of elevation. Unfortunately, as effective as that arrangement could be, the difficulties in maneuvering it also had their effect. Critics who dismissed the production as "all switchboard and no soul," as did Richard Lockridge of the *New York Sun* (November 3, 1938), might have thought differently had the technical operation been less in evidence.

Walter Ash has stated that he and Jean Rosenthal worked every night after rehearsals.

> It was fantastically difficult, because the lights never stopped moving. Each time the platform rose to a different level there would be a lighting transition, as well. And I don't mean just up and down either. There were all kinds of symbolic things: the cyc would go red, as if it were in flames; a low group of faces would be bordered, and then fade out; or a crowd would appear on another part of the cyc. All this was done with lights. Fade in, fade out, lap dissolves—just like a movie![1]

According to Houseman, the first reaction to *Danton's Death* came just ten days before the scheduled previews, when Marc Blitzstein brought the news that they were all guilty of a serious error and suggested closing down the production immediately. When Houseman refused, Blitzstein gave the reason why. The Moscow purge trials were still fresh in people's minds. *Danton*, it was feared, would suggest Trotsky and his persecution, while Robespierre was equally certain to be equated with Joseph Stalin.

The Party's reaction to *Danton* was a matter of the gravest concern for Blitzstein. He explained to Houseman that unless the production were brought into line it might be picketed. He insisted that a meeting with V. J. Jerome, of the local Communist Party, be held as soon as possible to discuss the matter.

At this meeting a few minor changes were agreed upon. The removal of a few of the more obvious Trotsky-Stalin parallels was sufficient to

Jan Tichacek's rendering for *Danton's Death*, which shows the set in its final position with the cyclorama split and the guillotine blade silhouetted behind Danton and his executioners. *Courtesy of Leo van Witsen.*

placate Jerome. Actually, the Trotsky-Stalin parallel was the least of the Party's objections. *Danton's Death* was clearly antirevolutionary, expressing profound disbelief in the ability of political institutions or revolutions to effect any form of social change.

An indication of the party line came early in the negotiations with Jerome. The *Daily Worker* (October 20, 1938) let it be known that Houseman and Welles were distorting "the history of the French Revolution as extravagantly as does MGM's 'Marie Antoinette' " and demanded that "the script be changed or the show dropped from the repertoire."

Richard Wilson and Walter Ash, the Mercury stage managers, disagree over how much actual pressure was brought to bear against the production. Wilson remembers the changes that followed (especially the St. Just speech, "which was tried out all over that script") coming as the result of "shall we say, outside suggestions?"[2] Ash, while conceding that the play "didn't end with St. Just because Orson wanted it that way," discounts the pressure as "a fringe thing, never a prime mover." Houseman offered a more realistic explanation: "Theoretically, at least, the speech was put last to end the play on a note that would please the Party; in fact, Orson was delighted to have a chance to bring down the curtain."

Judging by Welles's earlier productions, *Danton's Death* quite probably began with a coherent structure whose expressive framework made as lucid a statement as did *Julius Caesar* and *The Shoemaker's Holiday*. In bringing the production into line with Party standards this statement became manifestly wrong. Any attempt to rectify their political mistake would have required drastic alterations. Welles typically managed to imbed his expressive devices so deeply within a production's structure that the only viable way to alter its statement would have been to change the production concept entirely. These last minute attempts to standardize *Danton* only succeeded in leaving it without any message at all. Thus, while the Party withdrew its active support, it agreed not to boycott the production. As a practical matter, this proved not to be important. *Danton* was so badly received that it lasted for only 21 performances.

Danton's Death offended practically every segment of the Mercury audience. Considered solely on the merits of the production, it is hard to understand the level of emnity that it engendered. However, given the prevailing cultural climate of the 1930s, *Danton's Death* was an affront to its audience, whether that audience was avowedly Communist or not. The source of the trouble was that the production did not have a viable political message. Although the statements in *Julius Caesar* were hardly profound, their very presence, however naive, gave Welles's experiments with form the weight of truth. In not presenting any clear statements, *Danton* seemed empty and avant-garde. It struck the Mercury audience

Leo van Witsen's costume sketch for one of the gentlemen of
the Revolution. *Courtesy of Leo van Witsen.*

as elitist and esoteric, not at all the popular theatre they had expected to support.

Up to this point the Mercury's record had been outstanding. Yet, *Danton*, while it employed many of the same production methods that had characterized *Julius Caesar*, was soundly rejected. This, in turn, led critics and audiences alike to seriously question their assessment of the Mercury Theatre.

Richard Watts of the *New York Herald Tribune* (November 5, 1938) was among those who reflected this uneasy state of mind. He voiced his admiration for *Julius Caesar*, in both concept and execution. Indeed, Welles's editorial excisions had, for Watts, heightened the work's power and effectiveness, and he commented on how happily Shakespeare's drama fitted into its modern framework. Compared to *Caesar*, Welles's re-ordering of *Danton's Death* was a model of fidelity to the original. Yet, Watts found it necessary to sternly reprimand Welles for this production, saying that it had been used merely as a vehicle for the stage director.

Apparently for the critics it was perfectly proper to use a play as a vehicle for some socially acceptable sentiment, in which case anything and everything was permissible. But without this, *Danton's Death* could only raise the same critical concerns as any other avant-garde production. John Mason Brown of the *New York Post* (November 5, 1938) recognized that the theatrical devices Welles employed in *Danton* were not much different from those used in several of his earlier productions, and that they were used with equal skill. However, for Brown the total effect in *Danton* was too arty and self-conscious. Richard Watts similarly found Welles to be self-conscious and pompous in his direction. He thought that this was not only a great evil in itself but that it boded ill for the future.

It is an interesting commentary that with the production of *Danton's Death* the same qualities that critics had previously hailed, overnight took on the appearance of faults rather than virtues. None of these critics were known to be Communists. All were, however, strongly influenced by the prevailing cultural climate: art should be relevant and its message acceptable in terms of social and political ideals.

Underlying much of the criticism, clearly, was a response to the word "revolution," and the play's failure to present a readily understandable political interpretation of the issues it raised. However, there was a recognition of the effectiveness of individual scenes, even though Welles's expressionistic devices told a story quite different from the subjective content of the play.

It was not to be until *Citizen Kane* that Welles would again be able to successfully blend expressive form with substantive content. In *Kane*, as in *Julius Caesar* and in *Dr. Faustus*, form and content so interacted that each gave depth and meaning to the other. In *Danton*, however, all he presented was an exercise in expressionism that, finally, expressed very little.

With *Danton's Death* Houseman and Welles ended their participation in the "people's theatre." They had always considered themselves a production management unit quite apart from any particular project. They were quite ready to terminate any relationship with the Communist Party and with the Mercury Theatre, just as the year before they had severed relations with the Federal Theatre because it could no longer offer them proper support. The Mercury Theatre, which had been the center of their thinking and inspiration, and their springboard to fame, had suddenly become a burden to be disposed of so that they could go on to greater things.

By the summer of 1938 Houseman had already made a valuable alliance for himself and Welles with the Theatre Guild to produce *Five Kings* for the Guild's Subscription Series the following winter. They had entered the big time. So, while the second season might have been crucial to the survival of the Mercury Theatre, this would not necessarily have any effect on Houseman and Welles as managers. Houseman describes *Five Kings* as a "vaguely looming mass," altogether too big for the Mercury's tiny stage. Thus, there is little likelihood that this production was ever intended for the Mercury Theatre. As *The Cradle Will Rock* had been their ticket to Party support, so *Five Kings*, bolstered by the recent notoriety of "The War of the Worlds" broadcast, was to provide them with entry to the commercial theatre and, subsequently, to Hollywood.

9

Five Kings

Within three weeks *Danton's Death* had exhausted its audience, and not only the production but the Mercury Theatre closed its doors for good. As producers, however, Houseman and Welles still had one last, epic gasp ahead of them that season. But, after six cumbersome weeks on the road, *Five Kings*, too, failed ignominiously and was closed in Philadelphia by their coproducers, the Theatre Guild.

Houseman in *Run-Through* describes how this relationship started. It was early in May of 1938 (Welles at the time was twenty-three). Houseman and Welles had just had four successive triumphs; the Guild was having trouble in finding five plays to fill out its season; and, as Houseman put it, Welles and Houseman "offered to help them out." Welles and Houseman were to have complete artistic control and were to contribute $10,000 of the $40,000 projected budget. They were to put in $5,000 in cash and to contribute $5,000 in services. The Guild was to supply the balance.

They managed to avoid two very important questions that the Guild would have liked answered — how long the production could be expected to run, and how they expected to produce so expensive a show for so little money. These questions were to prove crucial when the rehearsal time turned out to be excessively long and to cost far beyond the agreed-upon estimate. Still, Houseman managed to forestall his partners, replying that the Mercury had its own inexplicable methods of production.

Houseman leaves the impression that he somehow bamboozled the Guild. In turn, the Guild management seems to have been inordinately willing to suspend their disbelief and abandon their usual procedures in hopes of cashing in on the (to them) mysterious aura of success that surrounded the Mercury Theatre. Had they examined the actual business practices of the Mercury they might have thought twice about this partnership.

The Mercury had always stretched its resources to the limit, putting the artistic requirements of a production before sensible fiscal policy.

Moreover, the cost of touring and paying union wages to a stage crew were considerations that they had not had to deal with before. Welles was accustomed to working in his own theatre, where both the facilities and a slave labor force were continually at his disposal.

The play finally went into rehearsal in one of the ballrooms of the Claridge Hotel near Times Square. It was then moved to the stage of whatever theatre the Guild could provide. The rehearsals themselves were undisciplined and erratic from the start. This was pretty much what they had always been, with Welles indulging in his generally unpredictable behaviour.

"J.D.B." of the *Christian Science Monitor* (February 17, 1939), who managed to penetrate the rehearsal barriers, described the way in which scenes slowly followed one after the other, with constant repetition and drilling. This, of course, was in line with the directorial techniques Welles had used in the past. However, there was one difference now; he had the Theatre Guild watching over his shoulder, and growing steadily more dissatisfied.

Welles made it abundantly clear that he wanted neither Houseman nor anyone from the Guild present at rehearsals. This could not have inspired much confidence, and half-way through the rehearsals the Guild expressed its disaffection by demanding the balance of the $10,000 that was still owed. This was real trouble, since Houseman and Welles had gone into *Five Kings* without any money, and were still in debt for *Danton*.

A more serious and immediate problem presented itself when the production was finally mounted at the Colonial Theater in Boston. The company arrived on the scene only to learn that their turntable had a faulty electric motor. In addition, they were faced with a situation that everyone had known about for some time—the fact that the second half of *Five Kings* had, literally, never been staged. Once again Houseman seems to have lulled himself into believing that the Mercury's former methods of operation would somehow work their magic under far different circumstances and that another of Welles's miraculous feats of ingenuity would save the day.

On the third day in Boston Welles announced that he would have to postpone the opening. There was nothing unusual in this request. *Macbeth, Horse Eats Hat, Doctor Faustus, Julius Caesar,* and *Danton's Death* had all been postponed an average of three times apiece. Unfortunately, this sort of luxury was over. Houseman explained to him, as he had in the past, that they were now in the commercial big time and that they had to meet the deadlines of a subscription audience. But even Houseman seems, at least silently, to have indulged in much the same kind of wishful thinking as did his partner. Since many shows were nowhere near ready when they opened out of town, he assumed that if it became absolutely necessary he could probably convince the Theatre Guild to give them another out-of-town engagement.

By all reports, the Boston opening was a disaster: The play had not had a complete dress rehearsal and ran, with two intermissions, till one in the morning. The reviewers felt that although the production showed promise, it was by no means a finished product and far from ready for New York. More important than the reviews from the Guild's point of view were the crew bills, which with overtime, amounted to over $15,000 and ran the production to more than $20,000 over the original budget.

For the Mercury, *Five Kings* posed an artistic problem, but one which they expected eventually to solve. The Guild took a very different position; for them *Five Kings* looked like a financial disaster, purely and simply. Lawrence Langner remembered the opening performance as being merely an interruption to the dress rehearsals. This impression of the production was largely an aftershock from the bills that he had just been presented with. All he could see were innumerable stage managers, their assistants, and Welles bellowing seemingly ineffectual orders at everyone.

After seeing the bills, Langner insisted that all-night rehearsals must cease. Houseman tried vainly to explain that Welles could work only by night and that the only chance of getting the show properly mounted was to let Welles function in his own way. Houseman tried also to explain the fine line in Welles's shows. After taking *Five Kings* to Washington and then to Philadelphia, the Guild undoubtedly felt that the line had been crossed and withdrew its further support.

Actually, despite, or maybe as a result of, all the wishful thinking and expense involved, *Five Kings* could have been on its way toward becoming a success. The problem was one of finding the time for more rehearsals. Welles tried vainly to work another miracle and get the big show going, but he needed time to get everything settled. The Theatre Guild apparently saw no possibility of this happening, and Welles, in turn, never got his extra time.

Welles and the Guild seemed to be at cross purposes. Their misunderstanding began early and failed to be corrected. In *The Magic Curtain* Lawrence Langner would have us believe that the Guild hoped to be rejuvenated by its "contact with youth." Apparently, he thought Welles would be an asset to go with the Guild's experience.

His first intimation of danger came when Jean Rosenthal showed him the projected plans for the revolving set. Langner thought that it would not be possible to tour the play with that set and advised Welles (through Miss Rosenthal) to design another, one suitable for travel. Had he realized that the set was itself the single most vital element in the production, Langner would probably have ended this misbegotten partnership right then and there. However, the scenic scheme was used in spite of his warning, and defeated *The Five Kings* in the end.

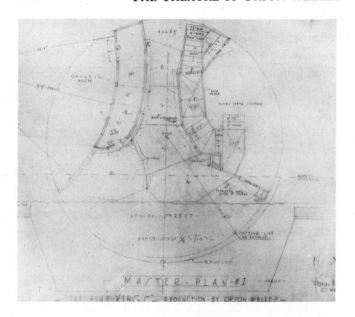

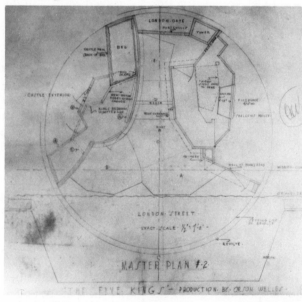

James Morcom's master plans for *Five Kings*. In addition, the production called for three platform plans. Overall, the scenery was divided into two parts: the "London" set and the various arrangements referred to as the "Battlefields." *Courtesy of James Morcom.*

Welles obviously worked in the belief that since the scheme was to be put into operation, the Guild would pay to see it realized exactly as planned. But, not understanding the nature of his production scheme, the Guild could not understand why Welles was unable (or unwilling) to cut it down to a more reasonable length. However, as Walter Ash, one of the production's six stage managers, explained, "moving and cutting weren't just a literary problem. There was also the technical problem of getting the transition right." This plainly required time, and the Guild was unwilling to allow the time or the expense it would have incurred.

It is conceivable that Houseman and Welles were being somewhat cagey with the Theatre Guild about their intentions, for while the overall scheme for *Five Kings* may have been formulated well in advance, the actual mechanics of it were only developed in production. This was a perfectly feasible way of working as long as Welles was directing entirely under the auspices of the Mercury banner. However, once the Theatre Guild came into the picture, it only fostered many of the disagreements and misconceptions that so marred their involvement in the production. The closing of *Five Kings* in Philadelphia showed a tragic lack of vision on the Guild's part. But that is not to say that they were solely to blame; neither Houseman nor Welles appear to have been at all helpful in explaining what they were about.

At no time in the theatre did Welles enjoy the work in his machinery more than in *Five Kings*, where it served him as both the physical representation of the world of the chronicle plays and, more importantly, as the expressive framework for his production. There was no attempt made to reorder his material into a tidy, if oversized, melodrama, as he had done with *Macbeth* and *Julius Caesar*. Rather, he tried to reveal the essential experience of the chronicles, as neither comedy nor tragedy, but as a moving pattern of events taking place in an ever-changing world. The rhetorical framework that tied these events together was supplied by a narrator who was removed from the action. The narrator, like a Greek chorus, maintained the play's continuity with only the highlights being presented on stage.

Welles had turned to Shakespeare, not merely for a reenactment of the chronicle plays, but in an effort to present a version—a summation, really—of their events as perceived in modern terms. Fundamental to the carrying out of his intentions was a technical fluidity that was rarely, if ever, attained. More often than not the production seemed, as it did to John K. Hutchens of the *Boston Evening Transcript* (February 28, 1939), "a ponderous marathon without style or particular point of view and utterly lacking in the magic with which the same Mercury Theatre once honored the Bard in the matter of *Julius Caesar*."

Apparently Hutchens, and his fellow critics in Washington and Philadelphia, were looking for the unifying element that had been readily identifiable in *Caesar*. However, in *Five Kings*, Welles chose instead to use the formal elements of his production, and not the content, as the basis for its expressive unity.

Critics in all three cities were quite sharply divided over it. Words like *novel, radical, innovative, ambitious,* and *herculean* were bandied about by both sides. Hostile as well as friendly critics noted the production's movielike technique. Peggy Doyle of the *Boston American* (February 28, 1939) regarded such features as "the chorus or interlocutor (Robert Speaight) in place of subtitles" as inspired; Philadelphia's J. H. Keen (*Daily News*, March 21, 1939) compared the kaleidoscopic effect of *Five Kings* to that of "an old-time motion picture of the days before the modern technique was ever dreamed of."

The fact is that Welles had no intention of staging a production that was better suited for the films. Instead, he deliberately used such techniques as fades and dissolves (all simulated with lighting) because they typified the modern outlook. When everything worked, the critics were quick to catch the significance. Thus, Nelson Bell of the *Washington Post* (March 14, 1939) observed that Welles, through his use of a revolving stage, "has found it possible to adapt a strictly motion picture technique to the requirements of a sound and comprehensive interpretation of Shakespeare. The mobility of the settings and the movement of the characters has been devised in such a way that the effect is one of continuous action and dialogue with a revolutionary blending of scenes."

There never was what might be called a "final" script for *Five Kings*. Fortunately, the working script is complete enough to point up Welles's intentions. Generally speaking, the scenes (32 performed of a potential 46) were quite short: the longest ran about nineteen pages, with several scenes of only a single page and still others consisting solely of stage business. The designation "scene" applied to a location on the revolving stage rather than to a unit of action.

Welles concentrated on the development of Prince Hal, first in his relationship with Falstaff, and second in his growing sense of responsibility toward his royal position. To be sure, there are scenes that reveal King Henry as a grieving father or a remorseful usurper. However, the action being highlighted rarely moved the plot along and was never dealt upon other than to accent the emotional state of the characters at any given point in the story.

A group of scenes, for instance, begins with the Percys confronting Henry over the matter of the Scottish prisoners, whom Hotspur has vowed to hold until the king agrees to ransom their kinsman, Mortimer. Not surprisingly, the king refuses even to have Mortimer's name mentioned in his presence again. This confrontation is followed by Hotspur extolling his grievances against his sovereign—grievances that stem from the fact that the Percys were instrumental in crowning Bolingbroke, a usurper, who now rejects Mortimer, the man that Richard II had proclaimed his rightful successor. Welles shows their conspiracy (with York, Glendower, and Mortimer) as being born out of a personal sense of abuse, and relegates its political significance to one rather brief passage by the Chorus.

Indeed, he seems to have carefully reordered the histories into a framework within which to disclose the personal stories of their participants. By far the largest share of *Five Kings* had to do not with matters of state, but with the common people. According to Walter Ash, this lent a "social significance to it. The common people were treated as human beings and made stronger and bigger than is normally done."

Central to Welles's understanding of the chronicle plays was his use of the character of Falstaff to completely dominate the stage. He was for Welles the production's major expressive element. The moving world that was created, and the events that took place on it, had more to do with the people that Falstaff represented than with the kings themselves.

While enlarging the stature and importance of Falstaff, Welles reduced the characteristics of Prince Hal that were considered typical of Shakespearean nobility. Even so, Burgess Meredith as Prince Hal felt that he delivered his first soliloquy splendidly, thinking himself at his best in poetic drama. Meredith apparently was not aware that Maxwell Anderson's grandiloquent passages in *Winterset*, in which he had made his reputation, were a far cry from the supple and varied poetry of Shakespeare. However, the difference was noted by the critics. Henry Murdock of the *Philadelphia Public Ledger* (March 21, 1939) found Meredith "lacking in poetic speech. . .the fact remains he is a modernistic Prince Hal, excellent in the intimate scenes but weak in the more orotund episodes." By comparison, Falstaff's presence was compelling, and humanity, in the person of Falstaff, loomed over the actions of the men of state.

Not all of the critics approved of this concept. Henry Murdock felt that Shakespeare had been played false by it, especially with regard to performance. Indeed, none of the actors seemed at all in character to him.

Walter Ash has said that Welles was interested in neither a typically grand Shakespearean production nor one "in the neo-realistic manner of present day Italian films." Instead, he (Welles) chose to characterize the human aspects of the chronicles, and their essential (as opposed to any specific) reality. Thus, the scenery was impressionistic rather than realistic in its representation of medieval architecture. *Five Kings* gave clear evidence of the Welles style, which was to come to full development in his films.

The expressive image of a world in motion was the equivalent in *Five Kings* to the cyclorama of skulls in *Danton's Death*. Individual scenes, however powerful in themselves, were kept within the context of this image. To a large extent, the action was thereby conventionalized

Welles as Falstaff, with Gus Schilling as Bardolph. *Courtesy of Hortense and Roger Hill.*

and used location and movement to suggest crowds and emotions. All of this led to a quality that many critics thought incompatible with Shakespeare —specifically, the element of caricature that they found injected into the plays.

The first scene in *Five Kings* takes place after the Chorus has read the prologue to *Henry V*. Further exposition of the affairs of state is limited at the beginning of the play to a brief one-page scene that depicts Henry IV as less than happy at receiving Richard's corpse, and subsequently proclaiming himself king. This is in the form of a dialogue between Exton and Bolingbroke, made up from parts of *Richard II* and *Holinshed's Chronicles*.

But the main business of act 1 is largely taken from *1 Henry IV*. Prominent in this act are the scenes surrounding the Gadshill robbery and its effect on Falstaff. Welles played up Hal's intentions of abandoning his low companions (act 5, scene 4) and the scene in which he and Falstaff act out the roles of the Prince and his father (act 2, scene 1). These two scenes are given great importance both in their length (vis-à-vis the other scenes) and in the fact that their completion necessitated several changes of locale not indicated in Shakespeare. This same importance is given to the later scene in which Falstaff, now penniless and racked with gout, is scolded by the Chief Justice (*2 Henry IV*, act 1, scene 2). Welles gave even further weight to the Falstaff scenes by combining both parts of *Henry IV*—specifically the scenes that presage the nature of Falstaff's relationship with the Prince.

The early Falstaff scenes took place before the "Basic London Set" of the revolving stage. These scenes were followed by a narration by the Chorus. During these scenes it was intended that the other sections of the revolve be reset so that in leaving the tavern, it turned not to the original London street, and then to the palace, but to a special unit for the Percy's house for a domestic scene between Hotspur and his wife Kate. Afterward, the stage revolved to the plains of Salisbury, a set that had also just been placed on it. Occurring at the end of the act, this radical alteration left the stage to be reset to its original arrangement during an intermission.

This is the sequence as it appears from the working script, which still was in need of much cutting if it was to come within the normal confines of the Broadway theatre. And it is interesting to note here a number of the scenes already cut from it. Immediately following the scene between Kate and Hotspur, Welles had intended one made up from parts of *1 Henry IV* (act 4, scene 2: Falstaff's recruiting philosophy) and *2 Henry IV* (act 5, scene 1: Fallstaff and Shallow choosing recruits). This was cut, as was a scene showing a despairing Hotspur at Salisbury with his lords. Welles went instead from the Percys' squabble to Falstaff's "Honor. . ." speech, and from there to the battle.

The only historical event shown in full is the encounter between Hal and Hotspur. This was given tremendous importance by Welles's staging of the battle sequence with the revolving stage in motion. Falstaff's "Honor. . ." speech, which precedes their conflict, serves as commentary on it.

In Welles's development of his script, the pattern of historical events (both dramatized and narrated) served as a leitmotiv to the main theme of the play: namely, how events emerge through the private actions of individuals both high-born and low. Thus, Falstaff's humbling by the Chief Justice was as important a scene, if not more so, in Welles's scheme of events as the formation of the rebel's plot. However, it should be remembered that the content of individual scenes mattered less than the expressive weight given them by their placement within the conceptual framework of the production as a whole.

There were two master plans for the London set. Both contained the same basic pattern: street-castle-street-tavern. When the production was working, characters could simply walk from one location to the next without being out of sight of the audience.

The revolve in its second position: James Morcom's rendering of the Council Chamber. *Courtesy of James Morcom.*

In the first act the major playing area within the palace was the council room, which was connected to the tavern by an alley at one end and a London street at the other. The interior of the tavern was shown in full, while its exterior and the palace wall made up the London street. This carried over into act 2, with the king's bedroom being inserted when needed. Now, however, the palace was connected to the tavern (whose interior was divided into its original area and Swallow's house) by London Gate and the Tower beyond.

It was impossible to cut any of the scenes at the beginning of act 2 without disturbing the general pattern of its revolving from palace to tavern to palace. Yet, in the urgent need to edit the script, Welles cut scenes without regard to the problems of maintaining the correct transitions between them. His concept of the chronicles was expressed as a pattern of movement. The arrangement of locations represented a summary view of the world as a whole, with transitions from locale to locale seen as the characters' progress through it. Any great leap forward (or back, for that matter) violated the natural unfolding of this concept every bit as much as did the production's finally insurmountable technical problems.

Act 3 was taken in its entirety from *Henry V*. The use of the Chorus to supply the historical narrative was extensive. The early scenes show the church's involvement in the forthcoming war between France and England, and the crucial encounter between the newly crowned Henry V and the French ambassador, who insults the king with a gift of tennis balls. These scenes are followed by Falstaff's death, and Pistol and his recruits going off to war.

At this point the arrangement of the set is changed. The entire revolving stage becomes a series of ramps and platforms representing the battlefields in France. Henry enters to deliver his "Once more into the breech" address, then receives the French ambassador (the same one who had earlier insulted him), who asks the king to ransom himself in exchange for the lives of his men. Welles's spectacular staging of the battle scenes (not referred to anywhere in the text) provided the expressive background for the war. The play ends with Henry's wooing and winning Katherine as his bride, and the Chorus's delivering the epilogue from act 5, scene 2.

Because of the magnitude and variety of the technical problems, Welles's production concept was not readily apparent. There were many scenes that were a credit to Welles's ingeniousness in grouping characters and getting them on and off the stage. However, there is little doubt that it was hard to follow this truncated *Henry IV* and *Henry V*.

Welles was continually being urged to cut rather than to add further content to his production. By the very number and brevity of the individual scenes, he could have been planning only a highly stylized experience. Through this style (or method) he tried to engage his audience with the

The revolve in its final position: James Morcom's rendering of the betrothal of Katherine of France to Henry the Fifth. *Courtesy of James Morcom.*

formal statement of each scene, while the content of that scene supplied the rhetorical frame of reference.

This becomes clearer if we consider a few of the scenes individually. Actor Martin Gabel, who saw *Five Kings* before it closed in Philadelphia, captured the essence of Welles's technique in his description of two disparate scene sequences. The first is the confrontation between Hotspur and Prince Hal.

It was the convention of Shakespearean productions, even the finest, for extras to run across the stage with battle flags and then have the two principals slash away at each other in high style. Orson obviously went to life for his idea. He must have imagined the medieval battle-fields as a sort of no-man's land, like in World War I, with everybody fighting over it and uprooting it and so forth. So, he had a single leafless tree for the scene, and a lot of mounds on the stage covered with tarpolin painted to look like Belgium after Ypres, or Mons, or what-have-you.

Then, Hal and Hotspur meet, and they didn't immediately leap into rhetoric. Now, if you've ever been to a prize fight, in the first round they feel each other out. One fellow throws a left, and the other blocks it. Gradually, they get an insight into each other's style and the fight develops. That's how Orson staged this scene.

The music began in tempo with the fight: a move, a feel-out, a parry, a thrust. Then, it developed in speed and intensity. In the meantime, the stage had started circling. Finally, upstage, half-hidden behind a mound, you saw Hal deliver the death-blow to Hotspur.

At this point, the revolve stopped; the music stopped; and there was a great moment of silence. Then, slowly, the revolve brought Hotspur around in front where he delivered his last words. The whole thing was perfection itself.

The second sequence of scenes, with the same kind of immediate visual impact, centered on Prince Hal's rejection of Falstaff. Gabel says:

He learns in the Tavern that Hal has been made king. So Falstaff says to his henchman. "He's my buddy. Follow me; we're in now." They start going Stage Left out of a door from the tavern, trudging to the Palace. The revolve was also going, in the opposite direction. That gave Welles time to create a whole kaleidoscopic effect with lights.

Finally, the palace comes into view, and there's Falstaff outside the gate with all the mob (as many people as Welles had). The guard tries to keep Falstaff out, but he gets through with his one henchman. Now, the Palace courtyard is raked, and as the stage revolves to bring it in front of you, two rows of nobles, all clad in ermine, come out of the coronation. The courtyard now occupies virtually the whole stage.

Falstaff breaks through the processional and goes inside. Then, he comes hurtling out backwards, followed by King Henry the Fifth, who delivers his famous address about rejecting the past and becoming a good king and so forth. After which, he exits with his nobles.

Falstaff is alone on stage, having been humiliated, and turns front in his shame. He then crosses over to his henchman and says something to the effect that "Well, he's just saying that *now*." [my italics] Wonderfully human! Brilliantly conceived! Not Henry Irving, not Beerbohm-Tree, not anybody could have done this scene as effectively as Welles did it.

Five Kings and *Citizen Kane* were close in time. They were also similar in many ways, not only in their common mechanics but because of the peculiar delight that Welles took in making the mechanics important and obvious. In *Five Kings* one was always aware of how he got from one scene to another; the order of events was artifically structured relative to the arrangement of the particular "world" as visualized on the turntable rather than to Shakespeare's chronicles. That this scheme worked at all was a reflection of Welles's great theatrical intelligence.

Pauline Kael, in *The Citizen Kane Book* (Boston: Atlantic Monthly Press, 1971), described the film as "a collection of blackout sketches, but blackout sketches arranged to comment on each other." *Five Kings* had very much the same quality. Welles's greatness as a director "was that he could put his finger on the dramatic fun of each scene." He probably had a more effective sense of melodramatic timing than anyone before him or since, in films or on the stage. Certainly, the duel between Hotspur and Prince Hal bears this out. The scene was structured so as to create the most powerful and immediate impact, and then ended abruptly as the climactic point was reached. And *Citizen Kane* had the same technique of sequences that stated their points, reached their climaxes, and swiftly made way for the next scene. This development also applied to *Five Kings*, since Welles intended it not as a conventional Shakespearean pageant but as popular theatre.

In Welles's hands this technique leaned toward expressionism. It invariably became the instrument of a kind of comic melodrama. This, not tragedy, was his vision of the theatre. And it carried over into film, as well.

The protagonist in *Citizen Kane* probably had more in common with Falstaff than is immediately apparent, and his story was almost as much comedy as it was tragedy. Welles directed *Citizen Kane* in such a manner that his hero's greatness became pomposity, with his enormous wealth visualized in strangely comic terms. Conversely, he tried giving Falstaff a tragic dimension, and played him not just as a low clown, but as a rascal with some dignity. Bringing Falstaff's character to life was another matter. For some critics that happened only once, in the scene where Prince Hal, now Henry V, regally renounces him. But the tavern scenes preceding this, which should have been sidesplitting, simply did not come off. In *Citizen Kane*, the failure to find tragedy proved a triumph, while in *Five Kings*, because the comic elements were not operating as expected, Falstaff's character merely seemed off-balance.

Citizen Kane was produced as popular entertainment. In the conception of *Five Kings*, this required reducing the content of the chronicles to a kind of theatricalized version of Classic Comics. What was remarkable was the form the production took. For the most part, Welles selected only those episodes which contained the most immediate and sensual appeal, and made them readily understandable to his audiences.

Pauline Kael considered Welles to be limited in his understanding of the character he portrayed in *Citizen Kane*. Yet she recognized that his shallow conceptions were offset by the other elements in the movie. So, too, the formal expressive elements in *Five Kings* carried it beyond the literal statements that were made by Welles's highly selective use of the chronicle plays themselves.

The production was contemporary not through its content but because of the way it made history understandable vis-à-vis the mass media of its day. Thus, the inhabitants of *Five Kings* were, in effect, the theatrical forebears of the pop characterizations of *Citizen Kane*. Everyone recognized the grieving father, the erring son, the rascal with a heart of gold. The "internecine conspiracies" of the chronicles might have been fully appreciated only by an audience already familiar with the original plays. But what Welles presented in *Five Kings* were those incidents which could be readily understood even outside their historical context.

Five Kings employed the same approach to its audience, the same techniques for engaging their emotions, that the "Voodoo" *Macbeth* and *Julius Caesar* had used before it. Had circumstances not prevented it, *Five Kings* might well have become an important event in our theatrical history.

John Houseman gives the impression that he and Welles had in mind a more or less straight, if colossal, production for *Five Kings*, to be a successor to *Julius Caesar* and *Shoemaker's Holiday*, but with a secondary motivation—to outshine Maurice Evans who had had several very successful Shakespearean roles.

The reference to Evans implies that, instead of a production that, in fact, had a great deal in common with *Julius Caesar* and *The Shoemaker's Holiday*, Welles was merely about the business of classical one-upmanship. Critics accustomed to mirror-image productions of Shakespeare did not approve of *Five Kings* and compared its acting with the acting of the Maurice Evans company and its production with the productions of Margaret Webster—all to the derogation of *Five Kings*.

The night before the Guild closed *Five Kings* in Philadelphia, Welles came in to New York in an attempt to raise the money needed to keep it open. He offered first to Tallulah Bankhead (whose husband, John Emory, was playing Hotspur), then to Marc Connelly, and finally to Sherman Billingsley his father's estate as collateral. (Welles was not due to inherit it until he turned twenty-five, which was still more than a year off). "It's his optimism I remember most," reported Marc Connelly. "He fully expected somebody to come up with twenty-five thousand dollars in cash at that hour of the morning." There were no takers, and in a telegram to his stage manager, Walter Ash, a by-now-despondent Welles could say only that he had failed to raise the money.

Welles steadfastly maintained that somewhere, somehow, *Five Kings* would be reborn, and for nearly twenty years the production remained for him in a Bronx warehouse. To be sure, he mounted two other productions of something similar to *Five Kings*—for Dublin Gate Productions in 1960 and in the film version, *Chimes at Midnight*, five years after that—but both lacked the scope and sheer magnificance of his original intentions.

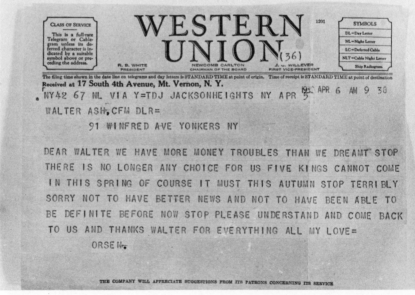

Telegram from Welles to his production stage manager, Walter Ash, following the collapse of *Five Kings* in Philadelphia. *Courtesy of Walter Ash.*

10
The Radio Years: 1934-40

The first thing that impressed Houseman about Orson Welles was his voice. This astounding instrument "startled not so much by its loudness but by its surprising vibration." At one of their early meetings Houseman asked Welles to audition for the leading role in *Panic*. It consisted of Welles's reading the character's suicide speech for author Archibald MacLeish. Both men were thus able to hear "that voice for the first time in its full and astonishing range."[1]

What Houseman is describing is a stage voice. Another, more acute, observation of Welles reveals the quality that made him so unique and defines the nature of his appeal as an actor. Houseman was not as impressed with the force and brilliance of Welles's voice as he was with its charm and courtesy. To this day when one hears Welles on the television narrating a special about the great white whale or the African baobob tree, one is struck by the magnitude that his voice gives to its subject. At the end of each performance Welles will say, as he always has, simply, "This is Orson Welles." These same four words were at the heart of his success on radio. After all the oratory, Welles leaves the impression of intimacy. The magnitude of his subject is finally a personal message to the individual listener.

This intimate quality is also central to radio as an artistic form, a form that Welles at one time (notably "*The War of the Worlds*" broadcast) was able to exploit to its fullest potential. He manipulated the devices of radio to make an artistic statement in much the same way that he used the devices of the theatre. *Citizen Kane* was, in fact, a summa of the devices of both radio and the theatre. All media makes an appeal to the senses. Welles discovered the basic formal qualities to maximize this appeal. The rhetorical content of Welles's radio programs, of his theatrical productions, and of his movies is special because it is so inextricably bound to the most heightened appeal to perceptions and sensations that each of these media can make.

Even before his first meeting with Houseman in the winter of 1934, Welles began his radio career on "The March of Time" series. The Dionne quintuplets had recently been born, and Welles was asked by the producer if he could imitate five different baby cries. (He and his wife, Virginia, marked the occassion by begging an advance from the show to splurge on a victory meal at "21"; however, they both looked so shabby that they were turned away.) Thereafter, Welles began to make weekly appearances on "The March of Time," playing such diverse characters as FDR, Haile Selassie, Hindenburg, Horace Greeley, Paul Muni, Victor Emmanuel, Hirohito, Charles Laughton, and Sir Basil Zaharoff. Within a year of his debut Welles could claim membership in that elite band of radio actors who commanded salaries second only to the highest paid movie stars.

Welles's considerable earnings as a radio actor, peaking somewhere between fifteen hundred and two thousand dollars a week, are evidence enough of his great demand with the networks. He fulfilled his many committments by "bicycling" from one studio to another, often arriving with barely the time for a last minute run-through before going on the air. While directing the "Voodoo" *Macbeth*, Welles commuted back and forth between Harlem and midtown as many as three times each day to accomodate his various radio assignments.

It was Welles's voice that assured his success as a radio performer. The extent to which his creative intellect figured into his early career in radio is hard to determine. From 1935 to 1937, he appeared mostly in shows over which he exercised little if any artistic control. (The possible exceptions to this would be the four-part adaptation of *Les Miserables* that he arranged, directed, and starred in for Mutual in the summer of 1936, plus his "*Hamlet*" and "*Macbeth*", each in two parts, for the Columbia Workshop in the fall and winter of that year.)

Despite Houseman's contention that Welles singlehandedly raised the whole level of radio acting, the decisive factor in his being awarded his own weekly program could hardly have been his considerable gifts as a performer. In fact, "the phenomenal offer" was timed to the success of the Mercury Theatre's first season. Welles could have the hour 9-10 P.M. EDST on Mondays for ten weeks beginning July 11, 1938. CBS agreed to sustain the show, which was also to be carried by the Canadian Broadcasting Corporation. The title given to it by the network was "First Person Singular," and the show called for Welles to write, direct, and appear in each episode and, as himself, introduce and narrate them.

The *New York Times* greeted the news of "First Person Singular" with the hope that Welles would bring to radio "the experimental techniques that have proved so successful in another medium." Touted as a prestige show of general appeal, the format to "First Person Singular" capitalized on the psychological study of radio that Hadley Cantril and Gordon W. Allport had written and published three years before. Cantril showed how demagogues like Huey Long and Father Coughlin had so effectively mobilized the unique qualities of this new medium. The wild oratory of the tent-show evangelist did not translate to radio, Cantril noted. Spellbinders like Coughlin and Long, realizing this, spoke quite differently. There was less bombast and more artistry to their presentations, less brute force and more cunning. Everything was directed toward the "invisible audience," toward making each listener feel welcomed to the charmed circle. A sense of involvement in these presentations was aroused.

> Friends, this is Huey Long speaking. I have some important revelations to make, but before I make them I want you to go to the phone and call up five of your friends and tell them to listen in.

Each listener is thus made a fellow conspirator, and their friendly attention for the duration of the show guaranteed. Long worked hard at doing away with formality and awe and elevating his listeners to a position of equality with even the highest officials. The way they presented themselves, their very manner and organization, was enough to assure Coughlin and Long that their audiences would likely believe them and think their simplistic and often dangerous solutions to the national ills perfectly valid. Cantril's findings showed that "a sound argument is always less important for the demagogue than are weighted words."[2]

That is not to suggest that Welles and CBS were aware of the Cantril study; however, in an interview with Richard O'Brien of the *Times* he also spoke of the "invisible audience." Whatever his source, Welles had certainly become aware of the first principle of his medium. "Intimacy," he told O'Brien, "is one of radio's richest possessions." He then proceeded to exploit the peculiar qualities of the medium for his own purposes as fully as Coughlin and Long had for theirs. "First Person Singular" made the drama as spellbinding as Coughlin and Long's political rhetoric — using pretty much the same devices, too. The most successful of Welles's broadcasts was, of course, *"The War of the Worlds,"* which proved that the manipulation of radio techniques (in this case, the weighted words of a news event) could lend a compelling logic even to something as far-fetched as an invasion from outer space.

Welles seldom paid the kind of attention to his radio program that he brought to the theatre. Thus, it is difficult to appraise — except for *"The War of the Worlds"* — just how he managed to animate the formal qualities of the medium to vitalize the rhetorical content of his productions. (Houseman credits him with inventing all sorts of "ingenius and dramatic devices." A full and comparative study of Welles's radio work, while invaluable, is really outside the scope of this discussion.) It is only because of the widespread attention that the Martian broadcast received that one is able to definitively link it to Welles's characteristic work habits.

Houseman and Welles were already an established partnership at the time of the CBS offer; therefore, it was only natural that Houseman began

Welles in his customary shirt-sleeves and suspenders directing a rehearsal of the "Mercury Theatre on the Air." *Courtesy of Hortense and Roger Hill.*

work on the script to their first show while Welles devoted his attention to other matters. As the "creative" member of this partnership, Welles was to supervise Houseman's efforts and direct the production. The decision was made to lead off the series with *"Treasure Island,"* but less than a week before going on the air Welles hit upon *"Dracula."* Houseman left off the earlier project and began the cutting and pasting for *"Dracula."* The sole surviving report of this broadcast is Houseman's reference to its innovative use of music as a radio signature (Tchaikovsky's Piano Concerto in B-Flat minor) for this and all ensuing productions.

The tenth and final program under the network's original offer was *"Julius Caesar"*; however, by that time CBS had agreed to sustain it an additional thirteen weeks, and "First Person Singular" was renamed "The Mercury Theatre on the Air." Acknowledging its growing reputation as radio's foremost dramatic series, CBS moved the show from Monday to prime time (8-9 P.M.) on Sunday nights. The first presentation in this new time slot was to have been a life of Vincent Van Gogh, but this was dropped in favor of *"Jane Eyre."* The *"Caesar"* and *"Dracula"* scripts are the only ones that Welles is known to have had any hand at all in writing. Otherwise, the first thirteen programs were entirely the work of John Houseman. Welles would discuss the tone and mood of the production with him, and Houseman would go off and write the script. The early rehearsals were directed by Welles's assistant on the show, Paul Stewart, with Welles himself attending to such things as timing and sound effects. The nucleus of these radio casts were drawn, in the main, from such Mercury Theatre regulars as Ray Collins, Eustace Wyatt, Joseph Cotton, Agnes Morehead, George Coulouris, Arthur Anderson, and "Anna Stafford," the stage name that Welles had chosen for his wife, Virginia, during their WPA days. Still, from the top of these broadcasts until Welles signed off with "Obediently yours, Orson Welles," the results, according to Houseman, were as much improvised as planned.

For their fourteenth program, *"Hell on Wheels,"* Houseman and Welles engaged a writer from outside their immediate circle, Howard Koch, who had come to their attention via the Federal Theatre grapevine. Koch's play *The Lonely Man* had enjoyed a considerable success at the Blackstone Theatre in Chicago, thanks largely, he admits, to the performance of John Huston in the role of Abraham Lincoln. The play attracted the attentions of Houseman and Welles. Discussions were underway for bringing *The Lonely Man* to the Mercury Theatre when Robert Sherwood's *Abe Lincoln in Illinois* was announced by the Playwright's Company. The Koch play was dropped, but when the awesome burden of keeping up this weekly writing chore became too much for Houseman, he was again in touch with Koch. Since CBS itself was underwriting these broadcasts, all Houseman could offer in the way of a salary was seventy-five dollars per week; however, the rights to any property that

Koch developed remained with him. (In the case of "The War of the Worlds" this has meant for Koch an equal share in the sale of some five hundred thousand record albums over the years.) One thing more: since the radio program, like his work in the theatre, was being promoted as an all-Welles effort, Koch could expect to receive no immediate publicity. Koch agreed to these conditions, and for the next five months—from "*Hell on Ice*" on October 9, 1938, to "*The Glass Key*" on March 10, 1939 —he was the writer of record for "The Mercury Theatre on the Air." (Koch quit the show to accept an offer from Hollywood. His successor was Howard Teichmann, who took up the weekly writing chore for the next two years.)

Koch followed "*Hell on Ice*" with "*Seventeen,*" "*Around the World in 80 Days,*" and then "*The War of the Worlds.*" It came with a message from Welles that "*War of the Worlds*" was to be a Halloween prank and that he wanted Koch to write it in the style of a news bulletin. For all the disclaimers, including several announcements that clearly identify it as a performance, the format for "*War of the Worlds*" was identical to a special events broadcast. It was, in effect, much like shouting fire in a crowded theatre; the audience would hardly mount a careful investigation before fleeing the premises. The more careful listener to "*War of the Worlds*" must surely have realized that the very sequence of events made it logically impossible; however, the fact still remains that thousands of people truly believed that the end of the world was at hand. This was the result of Welles's manipulation of an already established and persuasive formula.

The *Daily Worker* (November 3, 1938) attributed listener reaction to the liklihood that "Americans, in their imagination, substituted Hitler for the Martians." Whether or not this is the case, radio audiences had certainly become conditioned to having their favorite shows suddenly interrupted with news of some catastrophe or other. "*The War of the Worlds*" broadcast began innocently enough with the usual announcer's introductions. Nothing was said that might have alerted people to the Halloween prank that was to follow. Welles's opening remarks were on the order of a long, rambling history of how this world has long been under scrutiny by creatures who "are to our minds as ours are to the beasts in the jungle," creatures with designs against us. This was typical science-fiction pap and could hardly have made any special mark on its audience.

Welles's remarks were followed by an announcer who further delayed the dramatic excitement by delivering a weather forecast. At this point, however, an important, if almost imperceptible change was made. The weather forecast established the present tense. Simply but brilliantly, Welles had moved the broadcast from one of casual retrospect to the immediacy of current events. He then cut to a program of dance music by Ramon Raquello and his orchestra. This final deception in fact introduced Welles's central narrative line.

His theatrical productions were geared toward capturing audience attention from the start. He confronted them with violently expressive images even as they were taking their seats. The process in *"The War of the Worlds"* was much subtler. Its first few minutes were deliberately innocuous, even boring. Welles did not want to draw in his audience until exactly the right moment — a sudden break in the music to announce the sighting of several unaccountable eruptions on Mars. The news was kept very low-key: an atmospheric disturbance on a dead planet some forty million miles away. No danger in that. The second interruption served to play down even the suspicion that there might be living intelligence on Mars. When taken together, however, these two news bulletins, breaking in as they did on a previously scheduled broadcast (i.e., Ramon Raquello and his orchestra), left the impression of being unplanned and played on the same fears and growing concerns that radio audiences had come to attach to the real thing.

Welles, as if anticipating this sort of response, hones in on the Martian invasian through a series of fast-breaking news flashes. The first reports come from a Professor Pierson (played by Welles) of the observatory at Princeton, New Jersey. The landing is finally located in Grovers Mill, a few miles away and within easy striking distance of New York City. At this point Welles restated his dance-hall theme, just in case the audience had forgotten the show's carefully established framework. As yet the various "news" reports have all been within the realm of possibility. Not until some twenty minutes into the program, with the mobilization of the New Jersey State Militia, does Welles begin to escalate the sequence of events beyond a realistic time frame. Local residents, scientists, military men, even the secretary of the interior (sounding suspiciously like FDR), are interviewed continuously; and however fantastic their observations may be, Welles presents them to his audience as actual fact.

After the address by the secretary, the announcer returned to continue the report of ever-increasing disaster. The turn of the screw: the Martians were now attempting to paralyze communications and disorganize human society. Their war machines, rising as they did on hundred-foot metal tripods, were reported to be wading across the Hudson River to invade New York and — given the stated purpose of the show (i.e., a prank) — presumably, CBS itself. At the same time, mankind was depicted as being in a state of complete panic, scattering before the Martians' death rays and poisonous smoke. Neither our bombers nor our heaviest artillery could stem their advance. The carnage ended with a lone, anonymous radio operator calling, "Isn't there anyone on the air?"

The "middle break" occurred some forty-three minutes into the broadcast, during which it was again announced that the program was a dramatization and nothing more. The concluding few minutes of "*The War of the Worlds*" dropped the "news" format altogether. Professor Pierson (Welles) speaks aloud a bit of innocuous philosophizing and has an encounter with another survivor. Whereupon Pierson takes after the Martians on foot. Through the Holland Tunnel and up the Avenue of the Americas he walks until finally he locates one of their machines seemingly abandoned in Central Park. The Martians themselves lie dead on the grass, victims of our disease bacteria. They were, as Pierson notes, "slain, after all man's defenses had failed, by the humblest thing that God in His wisdom had put upon this earth."

In his book about the effects of the Martian broadcast upon its audience, Hadley Cantril wonders how anyone with a critical ear could have failed to notice that the show's sequence of disasters simply were impossible within the time elapsed since going on the air. Obviously, the average response to "War of the Worlds" was not intellectual; however, aside from the sort of internal evidence that Cantril points up, there was really no way of telling that the events themselves were a hoax. Welles's most outstanding formal device in this broadcast was the "realism" implicit in news bulletins and eye-witness reports; it provided him with the ideal expressive framework for his patently "unreal" content. It also could have validated even more outrageous content had Welles been of a mind to carry his prank any further.

Taking as a given that people thought it to be a news report at all, Cantril distinguished four types of listeners to the Martian broadcast.

1. Those who analyzed the internal evidence of the program and concluded that it could not be true.
2. Those who checked up successfully and learned that it was a play.
3. Those who checked up unsuccessfully and continued to believe that it was a news broadcast.
4. Those who made no attempt at all to check on the authenticity of the broadcast.[3]

It was the last two groups of people who panicked. Local police, newspapers, and radio stations across the country were deluged with phone calls of additional "sightings" or from people who were desperate to be evacuated to a "safe" zone. The *New York Daily News* reported over eleven hundred such calls within hours of the broadcast—more than they received at the time of the Hindenburg catastrophe. Over twenty families from a single block in Newark, New Jersey, fled their homes with wet towels over their faces to protect themselves against the poisonous gas of the Martian war machines. In Indianapolis, a woman ran screaming into a church: "New York has been destroyed; it's the end of the world." Services were dismissed. A Pittsburgh man returned home in the midst of the broadcast to find his wife, a bottle of poison in her hand, ranting, "I'd rather die this way than like that!" The call went out in San Francisco for able-bodied men to form a civil patrol to keep the Martians from crossing the Rockies. And Welles himself tells this story about actor John Barrymore, who, he says, was also taken in by the broadcast. Barrymore is said to have put down his drink, hastened out to his private kennels, and thrown open the gates for his dogs. "Fend for yourselves!", he declared and set them free.

There were countless other reports, many of them undoubtedly apocryphal; however, the reaction to the Martian broadcast was sufficiently deep and widespread to form the basis of Cantril's study on the role played by radio in the lives of different groups of listeners in the United States.

"The War of the Worlds" also gave rise to talk of censorship. The Federal Communications Commission ordered an immediate review of the broadcast. Senator Clyde L. Herring of Iowa announced that he planned to introduce a bill in the next session of Congress that would create a censorship board to which all radio programs must be submitted. But the end result, so far as Welles was concerned, was to provide his "Mercury Theatre on the Air" with enough notoriety to warrant the attentions of a sponsor — Campbell's Soup.

Normally, Welles's involvement in these broadcasts was totally last minute. In effect, he did the final polish. Koch insists that while "his work may have been brief, it was very important. He could do wonders in a few minutes." These were wonders of timing. But "The War of the Worlds" was an exception. From the first Welles knew that it could be a big show, and he devoted an unusual amount of attention to it. He conducted all the rehearsals himself and was meticulous in his supervision of every sound effect and musical interlude. Koch's script for the Martian broadcast was the perfect vehicle for Welles's particular aesthetic sensibilities, and with it he brought radio to a level of high dramatic intensity that is still without equal.

Welles came to enjoy the same dominating role in radio that marked each of his productions for the theatre (except for his run-in with the Theatre Guild). Naturally, he looked forward to the same control in his movie work, and he turned down a number of Hollywood offers before RKO dangled the irresistible lure of absolute creative authority over production. Welles was to exercise this authority only once in the movies — *Citizen Kane*. With *The Magnificent Ambersons* he began to lose essential ground. Thereafter, either studio interference or financial restraints would impede on his work. By the age of twenty-six Welles had seen the last of the winning combination: enough money and total artistic control. Losing this, his creative interest in the movies began to slip until there was nothing left for him but to join the ranks of Hollywood "hands."

The morning after the Martian broadcast. Welles explains his Halloween prank to the press. *Courtesy of Howard Koch.*

Appendix A
Cast Lists of the Stage Productions

MACBETH
by
William Shakespeare
Adapted and Directed by Orson Welles
Music orchestrated by Virgil Thomson
Settings and Costumes by Nat Karson
Lighting by Feder

CAST OF CHARACTERS

Duncan.....................(The King)..................Service Bell
Malcolm ....(Son to the King)..........Wardell Saunders
Macduff..............Maurice Ellis   Ross..................Frank David
Banquo ....Canada Lee   Lennox ....Thomas Anderson
Macbeth ....Jack Carter   Siward ....Archie Savage
First Murderer......................................George Nixon
Second Murderer ....Kenneth Renwick
The Doctor..Lawrence Chenault
The Priest...Al Watts
First Messenger ....Philandre Thomas
Second Messenger....................................J. B. Johnson
The Porter..J. Lewis Johnson
Seyton..Larrie Lauria
A Lord ....Charles Collins
First Captain ....Lisle Grenidge
Second Captain ....Gabriel Brown
First Chamberlain....................................Halle Howard
Second Chamberlain ....William Cumberbatch
First Court Attendant..................................Albert McCoy
Second Court Attendant ....George Thomas
First Page Boy ....Viola Dean
Second Page Boy ....Hilda French
Lady Macduff........Marie Young   Third Witch.............Zola King
First Witch ....Wilhelmina Williams   Witch Doctor ....Abdul
Second Witch ....Josephine Williams

COURT LADIES—Helen Carter, Carolyn Crosby, Evelyn Davis, Ethel Drayton,
    Helen Browne, Bruce Howard, Aurelia Lawson, Margaret Howard, Lulu
    King, Evelyn Skipworth.

181

COURT GENTLEMEN—Herbert Glyn, Jose Miralda, Jimmy Wright, Otis Morse, Merritt Smith, Walter Brogsdale, Harry George Grant.

SOLDIERS—Benny Tatnall, Herman Patton, Emanuel Middleton, Ivan Lewis, Thomas Dixon, George Spelvin, Albert Patrick, Chauncey Worrell, Albert McCoy, William Clayton Jr., Allen Williams, Halle Howard, William Cumberbatch, Henry J. Williams, Amos Laing, Louis Gilbert, Theodore Howard, Leonardo Barros, Ollie Simmons, Ernest Brown, Merritt Smith, Harry George Grant, Herbert Glynn, Jimmy Wright, George Thomas, Richard Ming, Clifford Davis.

WITCH WOMEN—Juanita Baker, Beryl Banfield, Mildred Taylor, Sybil Moore, Nancy Hunt, Jacqueline Ghant Martin, Fannie Subert, Hilda French, Ethel Millner, Dorothy Jones.

WITCH MEN—Archie Savage, Charles Hill, Leonardo Barros, Howard Taylor, Amos Laing, Allen Williams, Ollie Simmons, Theodore Howard.

CRIPPLES—Clyde Gooden, Clarence Potter, Milton Lacey, Hudson Prince, Cecil McNair.

VOODOO WOMEN—Lena Halsey, Jean Cutler, Effie McDowell, Irene Ellington, Marguerite Perry, Essie Frierson, Ella Emanuel, Ethel Drayton, Evelyn Davis.

VOODOO MEN—Ernest Brown, Howard Taylor, Henry J. Williams, Louis Gilbert, William Clayton, Jr., Halle Howard, Albert McCoy, Merritt Smith, Richard Ming.

DRUMMERS—McLean Hughes, James Cabon, James Martha, Moses Myers, Jay Daniel.

HORSE EATS HAT
by
Edwin Denby and Orson Welles
Based on *An Italian Straw Hat* by Eugene Labiche and Marc-Michel
Directed by Orson Welles
Music by Paul Bowles—Orchestrated by Virgil Thomson
Settings and Costumes by Nat Karson
Lighting by Feder

CAST OF CHARACTERS

Freddy . . . . Joseph Cotten
Mugglethorp. . . . . Edgerton Paul*
Entwhistle. . . . . George Duthie
Uncle Adolphe. . . . . Donald MacMillian
Queeper . . . . Dana Stevens
Bobbin . . . . Hiram Sherman
Grimshot, Lieut. of Cavalry . . . . Sidney Smith
Joseph . . . . Harry McKee
Gustave, Viscount . . . . France Bendtsen
Augustus . . . . Bil Baird
Myrtle Mugglethorp. . . . . Virginia Welles
Agatha Entwhistle . . . . Paula Laurence
Tillie . . . . Arlene Francis
The Countess . . . . Sarah Burton
Daisy . . . . Henriette Kaye

*Welles and Edgerton Paul alternated in the role of Mugglethorp.

Clotilda .... Lucy Rodriquez
Corporal .... Bernard Savage
Butler .... Walter Burton
First Footman .... Steven Carter
Second Footman .... J. Headley
Raguso .... Enrico Cellini
Berkowitz, a friend of Queeper's, in jail .... George Barter

WEDDING GUESTS—Ellen Worth, Arabella St. James, Marie Jones, Hattie Rappaport, Anna Gold, Myron Paulson, Wallace Acton, Pell Dentler, George Leach and Bill Baird.

TILLIE'S GIRLS—Peggy Hartley, Terry Carlson, Lee Molnar, Gloria Sheldon, Teresa Alvarez, Opal Essant, June Thorne, Mildred Cold and Geraldine Law.

COUNTESS' GUESTS—Georgia Empry, Solomon Goldstein, May Angela, Lawrence Hawley, Margaret Maley, Jack Smith, Mary Kukavski, Elizabeth Malone, Ann Morton, Helena Rapport, Helene Korsun, Nina Salama, Julia Fassett, Jane Hale, Jane Johnson, Michael Callaghan, Don Harward, Walter LeRoy, Harry Merchant and Warren Goddard.

CITIZENS NIGHT PATROL—Arthur Wood, James Perry, Victor Wright, Robert Hopkins, Craig Gordon, Harry Singer, Frank Kelly, Bernard Lewis, Henry Russelle, Charles Uday, George Smithfield, Henry Laird, Edwin Hemmer, George Armstrong, Jerry Hitchcock and Tod Brown.

    Horse .... Carol King and Edwin Denby
    At the Nickelodeon .... Bil Baird

DOCTOR FAUSTUS
by
Christopher Marlowe
Directed by Orson Welles
Music by Paul Bowles
Settings by Nat Karson
Costumes by Nat Karson and Orson Welles
Lighting by Feder

CAST OF CHARACTERS

The Pope .... Charles Peyton
Cardinal of Lorrain .... J. Headley
Faustus .... Orson Welles
Valdes (Friend to Faustus) .... Bernard Savage
Cornelius (Friend to Faustus) .... Myron Paulson
Wagner (Servant to Faustus) .... Arthur Spencer
First Scholar .... Willian Hitch
Second Scholar .... Joseph Wooll
Third Scholar .... Huntly Weston
Clown .... Harry McKee
Robin .... Hiram Shirman
Ralph .... Wallace Acton

Vintner . . . . George Smithfield
Old Man . . . . George Duthie
First Friar . . . . Edward Hemmer
Mephistophilis . . . . Jack Carter
Good Angel . . . . Natalie Harris
Evil Angel . . . . Blanche Collins
Spirit in the Shape of Helen of Troy . . . . Paula Laurence
SEVEN DEADLY SINS:
    Pride . . . . Elizabeth Malone
    Covetousness . . . . Jane Hale
    Wrath . . . . Helena Rapport
    Envy . . . . Cora Burlar
    Gluttony . . . . Della Ford
    Sloth . . . . Nina Salama
    Lechery . . . . Lee Molnar
Baliol . . . . Archie Savage
Belcher . . . . Clarence Yates
FRIARS . . . . Richie White, Jack Mealy, Warren Goddard, Robert Hopkins,
    Bernard Lewis, Peter Barbier, Henry Russelle, David Riggs, Henry
    Howard, Louis Pennywell, Harry Singer, Solomon Goldstein, Walter
    Palm, Pell Dentler, Frank Kelly, Charles Uday.
Puppets by . . . . Bil Baird
Masks by . . . . James Cochrane

The Music School of the Henry Street Settlement
Presents
*THE SECOND HURRICANE**
Music by Aaron Copland
Libretto by Edwin Denby
Conducted by Lehman Engel
Directed by Orson Welles
Lighting by Feder
Assistant Director, Hiram Sherman
THE CAST

Queenie . . . . Vivienne Block
Gwen . . . . Estelle Levy
Gyp . . . . Arthur Anderson
Lowrie . . . . Buddy Mangan
Butch . . . . John Doepper
Fat . . . . Harry Olive
Jeff . . . . Carl Crawford
The Teacher . . . . Clifford Mack
Mr. MacLanahan . . . . Joseph Cotton
Radio Operator . . . . Charles Pettinger
With an Orchestra of 20

*Premiered at the Henry Street Playhouse on April 21, 1937, and ran for a scheduled three performances.

THE CRADLE WILL ROCK
by
Marc Blitzstein
Production by Orson Welles
Conductor, Lehman Engel
Sets and Costumes by Ed Schruers
Lighting by Feder
Associate Procuder, Ted Thomas
Production Manager, Jean Rosenthal

THE CAST

Moll	Olive Stanton
Gent	George Fairchild
Dick	Guido Alexander
Cop	Robert Farnsworth
Clerk	Clifford Mack

Members of The Liberty Committee:

Editor Daily	Bert Weston
President-Prexy	Hansford Wilson
Yasha	Edward Fuller
Dauber	Warren Goddard
Dr. Specialist	Frank Marvel
Rev. Salvation	Edward Hemmer
Druggist	John Adair
Mr. Mister	Will Geer
Mrs. Mister	Peggy Coudray
Junior Mister	Hiram Sherman
Sister Mister	Dulce Fox
Maid	Josephine Heathman
Steve	Howard Bird
Bugs	Geoffrey Powers
Gus	George Fairchild
Said	Marion Grant Rudley
Larry	Howard da Silva
Prof. Skoot	Hiram Sherman
Prof. Mamie	Leopold Badia
Prof. Trixie	George Smithfield
Reporters	Robert Hopkins, Huntley Weston and Jack Mealy
Ella Hammer	Blanche Collins

Henry Colker, Rose Cooper, Georgia Empey, Harriett Flammang, Mary Kukawski, Donnald MacMillan, Jane D. Madison, Lillian Sheldon, Paul Varro, Ann Voorhees, Wallace Acton, Peter Barbier, Cora Burler, Solomon Goldstein, Edith Groome, Don Harwood, Frank Kelly, Paula Laurence, Elizabeth Malone, Aurelia Molnar, Walter Palm, Myron Paulson, Louis Pennewell, Helena Rapport, Henry Russelle, Nina Salama, Bernard Savage, Harry Singer, Raymond Tobin, Charles Uday, Richie White, Jay Wilson, Helen Brown, Helen Carter, Josephine Heathman, Lilar Hillums, Paul Johnson, Larri Lauria, Edith Miller, Clarence Porter, Ralph Ransom, Howard Taylor and Clarence Yates.

JULIUS CAESAR
by
William Shakespeare
Adapted and Directed by Orson Welles
Music by Marc Blitzstein
Sets and Lighting by Samuel Leve
Production Manager, Jean Rosenthal

CAST OF CHARACTERS

Julius Caesar . . . . Joseph Holland
Marcus Antonius . . . . George Coulouris
Publicus . . . . Joseph Cotten
Marcus Brutus . . . . Orson Welles
Cassius . . . . Martin Gabel
Casca . . . . Hiram Sherman
Trebonius . . . . John A. Willard
Ligarius . . . . Grover Burgess
Decius Brutus . . . . John Hoysradt
Metellus Cimber . . . . Stefan Schnabel
Cinna . . . . Elliott Reid
Flavius . . . . William Mowry
Marullus . . . . William Alland
Artemidorus . . . . George Duthie
Cinna, the poet . . . . Norman Lloyd
Lucius . . . . Arthur Anderson
Capurnia, wife to Caesar . . . . Evelyn Allen
Portia, wife to Brutus . . . . Muriel Brassler
Senators, Citizens, Soldiers, Attendants

THE SHOEMAKER'S HOLIDAY
by
Thomas Dekker
Adapted and Directed by Orson Welles
Music by Lehman Engel
Sets and Lighting by Samuel Leve
Costumes by Millia Davenport
Production Manager, Jean Rosenthal

CAST OF CHARACTERS

The King . . . . George Coulouris
Sir Hugh Lacy, Earl of Lincoln . . . . Frederic Tozere
Rowland Lacy . . . . Joseph Cotten
Askew . . . . William Mowry
Sir Roger Oteley . . . . John Hoysradt
Master Hammon . . . . Vincent Price
Master Warner . . . . John A. Willard
Master Scott . . . . George Duthie
Simon Eyre, the Shoemaker . . . . Whitford Kane
Roger, commonly called Hodge . .   Eyre's   . . . . Norman Lloyd
Firk . . . .   Journey-   . . . . Hiram Sherman
Ralph . . . .   men   . . . . Elliott Reid
Dodger . . . . Francis Carpenter

A Dutch Skipper ....Stefan Schnabel
A Boy ....Arthur Anderson
Serving Man ....William Alland
Rose, daughter of Sir Roger ....Alice Frost
Sybil, her Maid.......................................Edith Barrett
Margery, Wife of Simon Eyre ....Marian Warring-Manley
Jane, Wife of Ralph ....Ruth Ford

ATTENDANTS: William Howell, Charles Baker.
SOLDIERS: Charles Baker, Tileston Perry, George Lloyd, Frederick Ross,
   Frederick Thompson, John Berry.
SHOEMAKERS: Richard Wilson, William Herz, James O'Rear, Frank West-
   brook.

*HEARTBREAK HOUSE**
by
George Bernard Shaw
Directed by Orson Welles
Setting by John Koenig
Costumes by Millia Davenport
Lighting by Jean Rosenthal

CAST OF CHARACTERS

Ellie Dunn ....Geraldine Fitzgerald
Nurse Guinness ....Brenda Forbes
Captain Shotover ....Orson Welles
Lady Utterword ....Phyllis Joyce
Hesione Hushabye.......................................Mady Christians
Mazzini Dunn..Erskine Sanford
Hector Hushabye..Vincent Price
Boss Mangan ....George Coulouris
Randall Utterword......................................John Hoysradt
The Burglar ....Eustace Wyatt

*Opened April 29, 1938, at the Mercury Theatre. To make room for it, Houseman and Welles leased
another theatre on 41st Street, the National, where they continued to run *Julius Caesar* and *The
Shoemaker's Holiday* in repertory until *Heartbreak House* closed some eight weeks later.

*TOO MUCH JOHNSON**
by
William Gillette
Adapted and Directed by Orson Welles
Settings by James Morcom
Costumes by Leo van Witsen
Lighting by Jean Rosenthal
Cameraman, Paul Dunbar

*Opened at the Stony Creek Summer Theatre, Stony Creek, Connecticut, August 16, 1938, and ran
for two weeks. Nearly all record of this production, including the film footage, has since disappeared.

CAST OF CHARACTERS

Faddish . . . . Eustace Wyatt
Dathis. . . . . Edgar Barrier
Lenore Faddish. . . . . Anna Stafford
MacIntosh. . . . . Guy Kingsley
Augustus Billings . . . . Joseph Cotton
Mrs. Billings . . . . Ruth Ford
Mrs. Battison . . . . Mary Wickes
Purser . . . . George Duthie
Cabin Boy. . . . . Richard Wilson
Johnson . . . . Howard Smith
Frederic . . . . Erskine Sanford
Louton . . . . Louis Hefter

In addition, Arlene Francis, Jack Berry, Howard Smith, Augusta Weissberger, John Houseman, Marc Blitzstein and *New York Herald Tribune* columnist Herbert Drake appeared in the film sequences.

DANTON'S DEATH
by
Georg Büchner
English text by Geoffrey Dunlop
Adapted and Directed by Orson Welles
Songs by Marc Blitzstein
Settings by Stephen Jan Tichacek
Costumes by Leo van Witsen and Millia Davenport
Lighting by Jean Rosenthal

CAST
(In Order of Appearance)

Julie . . . . Anna Stafford
Danton . . . . Martin Gabel
Camille Desmoulins . . . . Edgar Barrier
Lucile . . . . Evelyn Wahle
Herault de Sechelles . . . . Morgan Farley
Philippeau . . . . William Mowry
Lacroix . . . . Guy Kingsley
A Lady . . . . Ellen Andrews
Robespierre. . . . . Vladimir Sokoloff
Marion . . . . Arlene Francis
Rosalie . . . . Ruth Ford
Adelaide. . . . . Rosemary Carver
Mercier . . . . Richard Wilson
St. Just. . . . . Orson Welles
Fouquier . . . . Eustace Wyatt
Barrerre . . . . Joseph Cotten
SERVANTS TO DANTON . . . . . . William Alland, Edgerton Paul, Stanley Poss
CONVENTION ATTENDANTS . . . . Richard Baer, Ross Elliott

MEMBERS OF THE CONVENTION, VOICES IN THE STREET: —
Sparke Hastings, William Herz, Stephen Roberts, Arthur Hoffe, Sanford Siegel, Fred Thompson, Ellen Andrews, Fay Baker, Helen Coule, Betty

Garrett, Victor Thorley, Robert Hanley, Kent Adams, Tyleston Perry, MacGregor Gibbs, Robert Earle, Wallace Lawder, Norman Wess, John Berry.

"Christine" sung by Joseph Cotten and Mary Wickes.
"Ode to Reason" sung by Adelyn Colla-Negri.

FIVE KINGS
by
William Shakespeare
Adapted and Directed by Orson Welles
Fencing under the direction of George Santelli
Music by Aaron Copland
Settings by James Morcom
Costumes by Millia Davenport
Lighting by Jean Rosenthal

CAST OF CHARACTERS

Chorus	Robert Speaight
Bolingbroke, later Henry IV	Morris Ankrum
Prince Hal, son to Bolingbroke, later Henry V	Burgess Meredith
Clarence, son to Henry IV	Richard Baer
Gloucester, son to Henry IV	Guy Kingsley
Henry Percy, called Hotspur	John Emery
Northumberland	Eustace Wyatt
Worcester	Macgregor Gibb
Westmoreland	John Adair
Warwick	Lawrence Fletcher
Exton	William Bishop
Vernon	John Straub
A Certain Lord	William Mowry
Archbishop of Canterbury	Edgar Barrier
Bishop of Ely	George Duthie
Lord Chief Justice	Erskine Sanford
Salisbury	Stephen Roberts
Bracy	Orson Welles
Bardolph	Gus Schilling
Poins	John Berry
Peto	William Alland
Page	Edgerton Paul
Gadshill	Sanford Siegel
Wart	Gerold Kean
Pistol	Eustace Wyatt
Shallow	Edgar Kent
Silence	Fred Stewart
Bullcalf	Stephen Roberts
Mouldy	William Herz
Feeble	John Willard
Shadow	James Morcom
Davy	Francis Carpenter
Court	Fred Stewart
Bates	John Willard

Williams . . . . Richard Wilson
Gower . . . . John Straub
Fluellen . . . . Edgar Kent
Servant to Hotspur . . . . Stanley Poss
MESSENGERS. . . . . William Bishop, Seymour Milbert, Robert Earle
King of France . . . . William Mowry
French Queen. . . . . Ellen Andrews
Montjoy, Ambassador of France . . . . Gerold Kean
A French Soldier . . . . Ross Elliott
Lady Percy, Wife to Hotspur . . . . Lora Baxter
Mistress Quickly . . . . Alice John
Mistress Doll . . . . Grace Coppin
Katharine, Princess of France . . . . Margaret Curtis
Alice, her servant. . . . . Rosemary Carver
French Lady . . . . Ann Saks

Appendix B
Selected Radio Credits*

1934-38	Acted in "The March of Time" series (NBC).

1935-36	Read poetry for Alexander Woollcott's show (NBC); acted in the "Cavalcade of America" (CBS), "Roses and Drums" (NBC) "Musical Reveries" (CBS), and "The Wonder Show" (Mutual) series; adapted, directed, and played Jean Valjean in a four-part show of *Les Miserables* (Mutual); and arranged, directed, and acted in "*Hamlet*" and "*Macbeth*," each in two parts (CBS)

1937	Occasional guest on "Standard Brands Presents" (NBC); narrated "*The Fall of the City*" (CBS); acted in the "Peter Absolute" series (NBC) and "Parted on Her Bridal Tour" (Mutual); and appeared as Lamont Cranston in "The Shadow" (Mutual)

1938-40	Appeared on "America's Hour" (CBS); acted a scene from *Julius Caesar* on "The Magic Key" (NBC); delivered a soliloquy from *Doctor Faustus* for the Allied Arts Testimonial special (NBC); guestesd occassionally on "The Edgar Bergen and Charlie McCarthy Show" (NBC); appeared in ongoing skits like "The March of Trivia"** for "The Fred Allen Show" (CBS); narrated, directed, and acted in "The Mercury Theatre on the Air" series.*** Beginning with "*Dracula*," the pro-

*Probably no one, including Welles, can reconstruct a complete list of his radio credits. Furthermore, this attempt has deliberately restricted itself to that time period which is the context of this study as a whole.

**From 1941 to 1942, a situation comedy entitled *The Great Gunns* was heard over Mutual. One of its characters, Lorson Snells, was of course a parody of Welles.

***For the first ten weeks this show was known as "First Person Singular" (which established its format of intimacy), then as "The Mercury Theatre on the Air," and from December 9, 1938, until it went off the air March 31, 1940, as *The Campbell Playhouse*. Throughout, however, it was very much a Mercury Theatre production.

grams in this series were "*Treasure Island*," "*A Tale of Two Cities*," "*The Thirty-Nine Steps*," "I'm a Fool" (overall title for three short stories), "*Abraham Lincoln*," "*The Affairs of Anatole*," "*The Count of Monte Cristo*," "*The Man Who Was Thursday*," "*Julius Caesar*," "*Jane Eyre*," "*Sherlock Holmes*," "*Oliver Twist*," "*Hell on Ice*," "*Around the World in Eighty Days*," "*The War of the Worlds*," "*Heart of Darkness*" (overall title for three short stories), "*A Passenger to Bali*," "*Pickwick Papers*," "*Clarence*," "*The Bridge at San Luis Rey*," "*Rebecca*," "*Call It a Day*," "*A Christmas Carol*," "*A Farewell to Arms*," "*Counsellor at Law*," "*Mutiny on the Bounty*," "*The Chicken Wagon Family*," "*I lost My Girlish Laughter*," "*Arrowsmith*," "*The Green Goddess*,"**** "*Burlesque*," "*State Fair*," "*The Royal Regiment*," "*The Glass Key*," "*Beau Geste*," "*Twentieth Century*," "*Show Boat*," "*Les Miserables*," "*The Patriot*," "*Private Lives*," "*Black Daniel*," "*Wickford Point*," "*Our Town*," "*The Bad Man*," "*The Things We Have*," "*Victoria Regina*," "*Peter Ibbetsen*," "*Ah, Wilderness*," "*What Every Woman Knows*," "*The Count of Monte Cristo*," "*Algiers* Adapted," "*Escape*," "*Lilliom*," "*The Magnificent Ambersons*," "*The Hurricane*," "*The Murder of George Ackroyd*," "*The Garden of Allah*," "*Dodsworth*," "*Lost Horizon*," "*Vanessa*," "*There's Always a Woman*," "*A Christmas Carol*," "*Come and Get It*," "*Vanity Fair*," "*Theodora Goes Wild*," "*The Citadel*," "*It Happened One Night*," "*Broome Stages*," "*Mr. Deeds Goes to Town*," "*Dinner at Eight*," "*Only Angels Have Wings*," "*Rabble in Arms*," "*Craig's Wife*," "*The Adventures of Huckleberry Finn*," "*June Moon*" and, lastly, a repeat of "*Jane Eyre*."*****

****Between the collapse of *Five Kings* in Philadelphia and his leaving for Hollywood, Welles toured the RKO vaudeville circuit as the Rajah of Rook in a twenty minute stage version of "*The Green Goddess*."

*****In 1946 "The Mercury Theatre on the Air" returned to CBS as a half-hour summer replacement for thirteen weeks.

Notes

N.B. Quotations by Welles himself come from the Hills' collection of Wellesiana. Individual sources for interviews have a corresponding note for the first reference in the text, but are uncited in the notes thereafter.

Preface

1. Maurice Bessy, *Orson Welles* (New York: Crown Publishers, 1963), p. 15.
2. Charles Higham, *The Films of Orson Welles* (Berkeley, Calif.: University of California Press, 1971), p. 191.
3. Andrew Sarris, "Citizen Kane: The American Baroque," in Ronald Gottesman, ed., *Focus on Citizen Kane* (Englewood Cliffs, N.J.: Prentice-Hall, Inc., 1971), p. 102.
4. Walter H. Sokel, *The Writer in Extremis* (Stanford, Calif.: Stanford University Press, 1959), p. 4.

Chapter 1: Early Welles, 1931-36

1. Michael MacLiammoir, *All for Hecuba* (London: Methuen & Company, 1946), p. 129.
2. A. P. Rossiter, "Angel with Horns: The Unity of Richard III," in Eugene M. Waith, ed., *Shakespeare: The Histories* (Englewood Cliffs, N.J.: Prentice-Hall, Inc., 1965), p. 68.
3. Ibid., p. 82.
4. MacLiammoir, *All for Hecuba*, p. 137.
5. D. S., *Irish Independent*, October 14, 1931.
6. *Irish Times*, October 14, 1931.
7. M. M., *Irish Independent*, November 4, 1931.
8. *Irish Times*, December 28, 1931.
9. *Irish Independent*, December 28, 1931.
10. *Irish Times*, January 13, 1932.
11. *Irish Press*, February 3, 1932.
12. Betty Chancellor Johnston, letter to author, July 2, 1972.
13. Ibid.
14. Thornton Wilder, telephone interview, Hamden, Conn., May 22, 1972.
15. Gertrude Macy, letter to author, September 19, 1972.
16. John Mason Brown, *New York Post*, December 23, 1934.
17. John Hoyt, personal interview, Los Angeles, August 18, 1972.
18. Brenda Forbes, letter to author, June 20, 1972.
19. Welles to Roger Hill, February 12, 1934.
20. Peter Noble, *The Fabulous Orson Welles* (London: Hutchinson and Company, 1956), p. 68.
21. MacLiammoir, *All for Hecuba*, p. 185.

22. Roger Hill, letter to author, April 15, 1972.

23. *Woodstock Journal*, July 19, 1934.

24. Claudia Cassidy, *Chicago Journal of Commerce*, July 14, 1934.

25. Judith Cass, *Chicago Tribune*, July 12, 1934.

26. Lloyd Lewis, *Chicago Daily News*, July 14, 1934.

27. *Woodstock Journal*, July 19, 1934.

28. Roger Hill, letter to author, April 15, 1972.

29. *Woodstock Journal*, August 23, 1934.

30. Virginia Welles Pringle, letter to author, October 22, 1972.

31. For a more thorough study of *Hearts of Age*, see the article by Richard and Rachel France in the February 1975 issue of *Film*.

32. Virginia Welles Pringle, letter to author, July 6, 1972.

Chapter 2: The "Voodoo" *Macbeth*

1. John Houseman, *Run-Through* (New York: Simon and Schuster, 1972), p. 184.

2. Norman Lloyd, telephone interview, Los Angeles, June 21, 1972.

3. In Margaret Barton and Osbert Sitwell, eds., *Sober Truth* (n.p., n.d.), pp. 49-50.

4. Stage direction in the Welles script.

5. Bil Baird, personal interview, New York, June 10, 1972.

6. Edna Thomas, personal interview, Brooklyn, N.Y., June 2, 1972.

7. Samuel Leve, personal interview, New York, May 29, 1972.

8. Hiram Sherman, personal interview, Westwood, N.J., June 1, 1972.

9. Virginia Welles Pringle, letter to author, July 6, 1972.

10. Virgil Thomson, personal interview, New York, May 31, 1972.

11. Henry Raynor, "Shakespeare Filmed," *Sight and Sound*, July-September 1952.

12. Ibid.

Chapter 3: *Horse Eats Hat*

1. Houseman, *Run-Through*, p. 207.

2. Edwin Denby, personal interview, New York, May 6, 1972.

3. Martin Gabel, personal interview, New York, May 30, 1972.

4. Wilella Waldorf, *New York Post*, September 28, 1936.

5. Marc Connelly, personal interview, New York, June 4, 1972.

Chapter 4: *Dr. Faustus*

1. Abe Feder, telephone interview, New York, April 8, 1972.

2. Wilella Waldorf, *New York Post*, January 9, 1937.

Chapter 5: *The Cradle Will Rock:* A Comment

1. Robert Warshow, *The Immediate Experience* (New York: Atheneum Publishers, 1970), p. 33.

2. Houseman, *Run-Through*, p. 255.

3. *Worker's Theatre*, May 1932.

4. Houseman, *Run-Through*, p. 267.

Chapter 6: *Julius Caesar*

1. Millia Davenport, personal interview, New York, June 3, 1972.
2. Jean Rosenthal, *The Magic of Light* (New York: Theatre Arts Books, 1972), p. 22.
3. Arthur Anderson, personal interview, New York, June 12, 1972.
4. Houseman, *Run-Through*, p. 296.
5. Rosenthal, *The Magic of Light*, p. 22.

Chapter 7: *The Shoemaker's Holiday*

1. Houseman, *Run-Through*, p. 329.
2. Lehman Engel, personal interview, New York, June 2, 1972.

Chapter 8: *Danton's Death*

1. Walter Ash, personal interview, New York, June 12, 1972.
2. Richard Wilson, personal interview, Los Angeles, August 19, 1972.

Chapter 10: The Radio Years, 1934-40

1. Houseman, *Run-Through*, p. 151.
2. Hadley Cantril and Gordon W. Allport, *The Psychology of Radio* (New York: Arno Press, 1935), p. 8.
3. Hadley Cantril, *The Invasion from Mars* (Princeton, N.J.: Princeton University Press, 1940), p. 88.

Selected Bibliography

A. Primary Sources

1. Personal Correspondence and Interviews

Anderson, Arthur. Interview in New York. June 12, 1972.

Ash, Walter. Interview in New York. June 9, 1972.

Baird, Bil. Interview in New York. June 10, 1972.

Bowden, Paula Laurence. Correspondence from Gennessee Depot, Wis. June 12 and 21, 1972.

———Interview in New York. May 11, 1973.

Bowles, Paul. Correspondence from Tangiers-Socco, Morocco. July 1972.

Connelly, Marc. Interview in New York. June 4, 1972.

Cotton, Joseph. Telephone interview in Los Angeles. July 9, 1972.

Coulouris, George. Telephone interview in Los Angeles. December 10, 1972.

Davenport, Millia. Interview in New York. June 3, 1972.

Denby, Edwin. Interview in New York. June 6, 1972.

Edwards, Hilton. Correspondence from Dublin, Ireland. July 24, 1972.

Engle, Lehman. Interview in New York. June 2, 1972.

Feder, Abe H. Telephone interview in New York. May 9, 1972.

Forbes, Brenda. Correspondence from Vineyard Haven, Mass. June 20, 1972.

Gabel, Martin. Interview in New York. May 30, 1972.

Hill, Roger. Correspondence from South Miami, Fla. May-September 1972.

———. Telephone interviews in South Miami, Fla. June 11 and August 13, 1972.

———. Interview in South Miami, Fla. December 22, 1972.

Houseman, John. Interview in New York. June 6, 1972.

Hoyt, John. Interview in Los Angeles. August 18; 1972.

Johnston, Betty Chancellor. Correspondence from Dublin, Ireland. July 2, 1972.

Leve, Samuel. Interview in New York. May 29, 1972.

Lloyd, Norman. Telephone interview in Los Angeles. June 21, 1972.

MacLeish, Archibald. Telephone interview in North Conway, Mass. June 1, 1972.

Macy, Gertrude. Correspondence from Snedens Landing, N. Y. September 19, 1972.

Morcom, James. Interview in New York. June 7, 1972.

Pringle, Virginia Welles. Correspondence from London. June 25 and July 6, 1972.

_____. Interview in New York. May 11, 1973.

Rosenthal, Theodore. Interview in New York. May 29, 1973.

Sherman, Hiram. Interview in Westwood, N. J. June 9, 1972.

Thomas, Edna. Interview in New York. June 2, 1972.

Thomson, Virgil. Interview in New York. May 31, 1972.

Weissberger, Arnold. Interview in New York. June 5, 1972.

Wilder, Isabel. Correspondence from Hamden, Conn. May 22, 1972.

Wilder, Thornton. Telephone Interview in Hamden, Conn. May 10, 1972.

Wilson, Richard. Interview in Los Angeles. August 19, 1972.

Witsen, Leo, van. Interview in New York. June 8, 1972.

2. Autobiographies, Letters, and Personal Commentary

Cobos, Juan; Rubio, Miquel; and Pruneda, J. A. "A Trip to Don Quixoteland." *Cahiers du Cinema*, no. 5 (September 1966).

Feder, Abe H. "Dialogues with Light." Unpublished lecture.

Grigs, Derrick. "Conversations at Oxford." *Sight and Sound*, Spring 1960.

Hill, Roger. Correspondence with Orson Welles. Woodstock, Illinois. August-December 1931, and March-June 1934.

Hoyt, John. "Fifty Cents Is Two Martinis." Unpublished manuscript.

Koval, Francis. "An Interview with Orson Welles." *Sight and Sound*, December 1950.

Silverman, Dore. "Odd Orson: An Interview." *You Magazine*, July-August 1951.

Welles, Orson. Unpublished diary. Ireland. September-October 1931.

_____. American correspondence with Roger Hill. March-June 1934.

_____. Correspondence to Katharine Cornell. Indianapolis, Ind. March 30, 1934.

_____. Correspondence with Whitford Kane. Spring 1934.

_____. Irish correspondence with Roger Hill. August-December 1931.

_____. "The Third Audience." *Sight and Sound*, Winter 1954.

_____. "Welles on Falstaff." *Cahiers du Cinema*, December 1967.

3. Plays

Blitzstein, Marc. *The Cradle Will Rock*. New York: Random House, 1938.

Büchner, Georg. *Danton's Death*. In Geoffrey Dunlop, trans, *The Plays of Georg Büchner*. New York: Irving Ravin, 1928.

Copland, Aaron, and Denby, Edwin. *The Second Hurricane*. New York: Boosey & Hawkes, n.d.

Dekker, Thomas. *The Shoemaker's Holiday.* In *Eight Famous Elizabethan Plays.* Edited by E. C. Dunn. New York: The Modern Library, 1932.

Denby, Edwin, and Welles, Orson. *Horse Eats Hat.* Unpublished manuscript. From *Un Chapeau de paille d'Italie* [*An Italian Straw Hat*] by Eugene Labiche and Marc-Michel.

Gillette, William. *Too Much Johnson.* New York: Samuel French, 1899.

Hill, Roger, and Welles, Orson. *Marching Song.* Unpublished manuscript.

Kingsley, Sidney. *Ten Million Ghosts.* Unpublished manuscript.

MacLeish, Archibald. *Panic.* New York: Houghton Mifflin, 1935.

Marlowe, Christopher. *The Tragical History of Doctor Faustus.* In *Eight Famous Elizabethan Plays.* Edited by E. C. Dunn. New York: The Modern Library, 1932.

Shakespeare, William. *Julius Caesar.* Baltimore, Md.: Penguin Books, 1971.

———. *Macbeth.* Baltimore, Md.: Penguin Books, 1956.

Shaw, George Bernard. *Heartbreak House.* In *Four Plays by Bernard Shaw.* New York: The Modern Library, 1953.

Welles, Orson. *Brite Lucifer.* Unpublished manuscript.

———. *Five Kings.* Unpublished manuscript. Compiled from Shakespeare's *Richard II, I Henry IV, II Henry IV* and *Henry V.*

———. *Winter of Discontent.* Unpublished manuscript. Compiled from Shakespeare's *II Henry IV* and *Richard III.*

4. Recordings

Blitzstein, Marc. *The Cradle Will Rock.* Musicraft Recordings 18.

———. *Marc Blitzstein Presents.* Spoken Arts Records 717.

Copland, Aaron. *The Second Hurricane.* Columbia Records ML5581.

Shakespeare, William. *The Mercury Shakespeare's "Julius Caesar."* Columbia Masterworks. Set C-10.

———. *The Mercury Shakespeare's "Macbeth."* Columbia Masterworks. Set C-33.

———. *The Mercury Shakespeare's "Merchant of Venice."* Columbia Masterworks. Set C-6.

———. *The Mercury Shakespeare's "Twelfth Night."* Columbia Masterworks. Set C-7.

5. Miscellaneous

The Crawford Theatre Collection. Yale University. New Haven, Conn.

Harvard College Library Theatre Collection. Cambridge, Mass.

Hill, Roger. Private collection of Wellesiana.

———. *The Todd School Handbook.* Woodstock, Ill.: The Todd Press, n.d.

Department of Special Collections. University of Chicago. Chicago, Ill.

Periodicals Archives. Irish National Library. Dublin, Ireland.

Theatre Collection. Library and Museum of Performing Arts. New York.

Theatre Guild Repository. Yale University. New Haven, Conn.

The Todd School. A student handbook. Woodstock, Ill.: The Todd Press, n.d.

William Vance Film Repository. Greenwich Public Library. Greenwich, Conn.

Wisconsin Center for Theatre Research. University of Wisconsin. Madison, Wis.

B. Books

Bessy, Maurice. *Orson Welles: An Investigation into his Films and Philosophy*. New York: Crown Publishers, 1971.

Buxton, Frank, and Owen, Bill. *Radio's Golden Age: 1920-50*. New York: Viking Press, 1966.

Cantril, Hadley, and Allport, Gordon W. *The Psychology of Radio*. New York: Arno Press, 1935.

Cantril, Hadley. *The Invasion from Mars*. Princeton, N. J.: Princeton University Press, 1940.

Clurman, Harold. *The Fervent Years*. New York: Hill and Wang, 1957.

Cornell, Katharine. *I Wanted to Be an Actress*. New York: Randon House, 1938.

Cowie, Peter. *The Cinema of Orson Welles*. London: A. Zwemmer Limited, 1965.

Edwards, Hilton. *The Mantle of Harlequin*. Dublin: Progress House, 1958.

Flanagan, Hallie. *Arena*. New York: Duell, Sloan & Pearce, 1940.

Fowler, Roy A. *Orson Welles*. London: Pendulum Publications, 1946.

Gorelik, Mordecai. *New Theatres for Old*. New York: E. P. Dutton & Company, 1962.

Gottesman, Ronald, *Focus on Citizen Kane*. Englewood Cliffs, N. J.: Prentice-Hall, 1971.

Griffith, Richard, and Mayer, Arthur. *The Movies*. New York: Bonanza Books, 1957.

Higham, Charles. *The Films of Orson Welles*. Berkeley, Calif.: University of California Press, 1971.

Hill, Roger. *A Handbook for Teachers*. New York: Harper & Bros., 1939.

Himelstein, Morgan Y. *Drama Was a Weapon: The Left-Wing Theatre in New York, 1929-1941*. New Brunswick, N. J.: Rutgers University Press, 1963.

Hosley, Richard, ed. *Shakespeare's Holinshed*. New York: Capricorn Books, 1968.

Houseman, John. *Run-Through*. New York: Simon and Schuster, 1972.

Isaacs, Edith J. R. *The Negro in the American Theatre*. New York: Theatre Arts, Inc., 1947.

Kael, Pauline. *The Citizen Kane Book*. Boston: Little, Brown and Company, 1972.

Kauffmann, Stanley, ed. *American Film Criticism from the Beginnings to "Citizen Kane."* New York: Liveright, 1972.

Langner, Lawrence. *The Magic Curtain*. New York: E. P. Dutton & Company, 1951.

Lindenberger, Herbert. *Georg Büchner*. Cardondale, Ill.: Southern Illinois University Press, 1964.

MacLiammoir, Micheal. *All for Hecuba*. London: Methuen & Company, 1946.

————. *Put Money in Thy Purse*. London: Methuen & Company, 1952.

Manvell, Roger. *Shakespeare and the Film*. New York: Praeger Publishers, 1971.

Mathews, Jane deHart. *The Federal Theatre*. Princeton, N. J.: Princeton University Press, 1967.

McClintic, Gutherie. *Me and Kit*. Boston: Little, Brown & Company, 1955.

Mussand, Joseph. *The American Drama, 1930-1940*. New York: Modern Drama Chapbooks, 1941.

Noble, Peter. *The Fabulous Orson Welles*. London: Hutchinson and Company, 1956.

Rosenthal, Jean. *The Magic of Light*. New York: Theatre Arts Books, 1972.

Seldes, Gilbert. *The Seven Lively Arts*. New York: The Sagamore Press, 1957.

Simon, Rita James, ed. *As We Saw The Thirties: Essays on Social and Political Movements of a Decade*. Chicago: University of Illinois Press, 1967.

Sokel, Walter H. *The Writer in Extremis*. Stanford, Calif.: Stanford University Press, 1959.

Thomson, Virgil. *The Musical Scene*. New York: Alfred A. Knopf, 1945.

————. *Music Right and Left*. New York: Henry Holt & Company, 1951.

————. *Virgil Thomson*. New York: Alfred A. Knopf, 1966.

Waith, Eugene M., ed. *Shakespeare: The Histories*. Englewood Cliffs, N. J.: Prentice-Hall, 1965.

Warshow, Robert. *The Immediate Experience*. New York: Atheneum Publishers, 1970.

C. Periodicals

1. Historical Articles

Anonymous. "*Winged Gorilla*." *New Statesman* and *Nation,* January 21, 1956.

Atkinson, Brooks. "The Federal Theatre." *New York Times*, May 2, 1937.

Billard, Pierre. "Chimes at Midnight." *Sight and Sound*, Spring 1965.

Blitzstein, Marc. "On Writing Music for the Theatre." *Modern Music* 15, no. 2 (January-February 1937).

"Checklist 10—Orson Welles." *Monthly Film Bulletin.* (London), January-February 1964.

Clay, Jean. "Orson Welles." *Realities*, no. 201 (1962).

Cobos, Juan, and Rubio, Miguel. "Welles and Falstaff." *Sight and Sound*, Autumn 1966.

Comolli, Jean-Louis. "Jack le Fataliste." *Cahiers du Cinema*, December 1967.

Daney, Serge. "Welles in Power." *Cahiers du Cinema*, December 1967.

"Drama Festival Draws Gay City Crowd to 'Trilby.' " *Woodstock Daily Sentinel*, July 13, 1934.

Ferguson, Otis. "Citizen Welles." *New Republic*, June 2, 1941.

"Five Thousand in Harlem Storm Theatre to see 'Macbeth.' " *New York Herald-Tribune*, April 15, 1936.

Flanagan, Hallie. "The Federal Theatre." *Saturday Review*, October 1937.

_____. "Spotlight on the Federal Theatre." *TAC Magazine*, January 1939.

_____. "These Are the People." *New Republic*, October 18, 1939.

Ginsberg, Walter. "How Helpful Are Shakespeare Recordings?" *English Journal*, April 1940.

Hampton, Morton, and Cammer, Eugenia. "Broadway Whiz." *Champion of Youth Magazine*, May 1937.

Higham, Charles. "Special Report: Citizen Kane Remembered." *Action* 4, no. 3 (May-June 1969).

Hillyer, Katherine. "Theater Guild and Welles May PHFFT, It's Reported." *The Washington Daily News*, March 18, 1939.

Houseman, John. "Again—A People's Theatre." *The Daily Worker*, September 18, 1937.

_____. "The Birth of the Mercury Theatre." *Educational Theatre Journal* 24, no. 1 (March 1972).

Johnston, Alva, and Smith, Fred. "How to Raise a Child." *Saturday Evening Post*, February 3, 1940.

Johnson, William. "Of Time and Loss." *Film Quarterly*, Fall 1967.

Karson, Nat. "Costume Sketches for Macbeth." *Federal Theatre Magazine* 1, no. 5 (April 1936).

Labarthe, Andre. "My Name Is Orson Welles." *Cahiers du Cinema*, no. 117 (March 1961).

Langner, Lawrence. "Future of the Government in the Theatre." *Yale Review* 27 (1937).

Lean, Tangye. "Pre-War Citizen." *Horizon* 4 (November 1941).

Leonard, Harold. "Notes on Macbeth." *Sight and Sound*, March 1950.

MacLiammoir, Micheal. "Orson Welles." *Sight and Sound*, Summer 1952.

Manning, Joseph. "The Federal Theatre Presents." *New Theatre*, March 1936.

Margot, Jr. "Woodstock, Illinois, Never Saw Equal of Last Night's Doings in All Its Mellowing Century." *Chicago Daily News*, July 13, 1934.

Meredith, Burgess. "Of Times, People and Mores in Films and the Theatre." *Daily Variety*, October 1970.

Murrow, Edward R. "A letter to (Miss) Willson Whitman." *The Stage*, July 1936.

"Orson Welles Discusses Association With F.T.P. at Shakespeare Society." *Hunter College Bulletin*, March 8, 1937.

Powell, Anne. "A People's Theatre." *London Studio* 16 (1938).

Powell, Dilys. "The Life and Opinions of Orson Welles." *Sunday Times* (London), February 3, 1963.

Raynor, Henry. "Shakespeare Filmed." *Sight and Sound*, Fall 1952.

Rosenthal, Jean. "Five Kings." *Theatre Arts Magazine*, June 1939.

"Shadow to Shakespeare, Shoemaker to Shaw." *Time*, May 9, 1938.

"Skit on 'Kings' Hit of Show." *The Journal-News* (Nyack, N. Y.), September 17, 1938.

Smith, J. F. "The Federal Theatre." *The Stage*, August 17, 1939.

"Theatre Festival Players Will Stage Hamlet." *The Woodstock Journal*, July 19, 1934.

"Theater Festival to Open July 12 at Opera House." *The Woodstock Journal*, July 5, 1934.

Thomas, J. G. "The Federal Theatre Project." Master's thesis, Columbia University, 1958.

Thomson, Virgil. "W.P.A. Shows with Music." *Modern Music*, November-December 1936.

Tyler, Parker. "Orson Welles and the Big Experimental Film Cult." *Film Culture*, no. 29 (Summer 1963).

Tynan, Kenneth. "Orson Welles." *Show Magazine*, October-November 1961.

_____. "The World of Orson Welles." *Observer Review*, April 2, 1967. (Originally appeared in *Playboy*.)

Waldorf, Wilella. "Mercury Plans West Coast Tryout for 'Five Kings.' " *New York Post*, May 4, 1938.

"Welles Explains Why the Actors Chose Woodstock." *The Woodstock Journal*, August 9, 1934.

Whipple, Sidney B. "Definite Program Mercury's Need." *New York World-Telegram*, April 15, 1939.

2. Dramatic Criticism

Anderson, John. " 'Danton's Death' Opens at Mercury Theatre." *New York Journal American*, November 3, 1939.

_____. " 'Julius Caesar' Brings Brilliant Life to Bard." *New York Journal American*, November 21, 1937.

_____. "Shavian Thunder Roars in 'Heartbreak House.' " *New York Journal American*, April 30, 1938.

_____. " 'Shoemaker's Holiday' Gay, Imaginative." *New York Journal American*, January 1, 1939.

Atkinson, Brooks. "Gotham Hobgoblin." *New York Times*, November 7, 1938.

_____. "Macbeth: Harlem Boy Goes Wrong." *New York Times*, April 15, 1936.

_____. "MacLeish's Panic." *New York Times*, March 16, 1935.

_____. "Marlowe's 'Tragical History of Doctor Faustus' Put On at the Federal Theatre." *New York Times*, January 9, 1937.

_____. "Mercury Theatre Adds Dekker's 'The Shoemaker's Holiday' to its Repertory." *New York Times*, January 3, 1938.

_____. "Mercury Theatre Opens with a Version of 'Julius Caesar' in Modern Dress." *New York Times*, November 12, 1937.

_____. "Mercury Theatre Reopens with Orson Welles' Production of 'Danton's Death.' " *New York Times*, November 3, 1938.

_____. "Mercury Theatre Restores Goerge Bernard Shaw's 'Heartbreak House' to the Stage." *New York Times*, April 30, 1938.

_____. "Sidney Kingsley Attacking the Munitions Manufacturers in 'Ten Million Ghosts.' " *New York Times*, October 25, 1936.

"At the Elliot." *New York American*, September 28, 1936.

B. B. "Doctor Faustus." *Nation*, January 23, 1937.

_____. "Horse Eats Hat." *Nation*, October 10, 1936.

Bell, Nelson B. " 'Five Kings' is Drama of Unique Design." *Washington Post*, March 14, 1939.

Broun, Heywood. "Shoot the Works." *New Republic,* December 29, 1937.

Brown, John Mason. "A Not So Voodoo 'Macbeth' Performed in Harlem." *New York Evening Post*, April 15, 1936.

_____. "The French Revolution in Two Recent Productions." *New York Post*, November 5, 1938.

_____. " 'Julius Caesar' in an Absorbing Production." *New York Post*, November 12, 1937.

_____. "Once Again Harlem's Voodoo 'Macbeth.' " *New York Evening Post*, April 18, 1936.

_____. " 'Shoemaker's Holiday' Produced at the Mercury." *New York Post*, January 3, 1938.

Cambridge, John. " 'Danton's Death' Leans Heavily on Personal Conflict." *Daily Worker*, November 4, 1938.

Carmody, Jay. "Orson Welles' 'Five Kings' Is Vital, Living Drama." *Washington Evening Star*, March 14, 1939.

Cassidy, Claudia. "The Drama, Like Green Fields, Lies Far Away." *Chicago Journal of Commerce*, July 14, 1934.

_____. " 'Hamlet' at Woodstock Stirs Chicago Interest." *Chicago Journal of Commerce*, July 28, 1934.

_____. "Woodstock's Last Play. . . ." *Chicago Journal of Commerce*, August 11, 1934.

Chapman, John, " 'Horse Eats Hat' Is Mad But Not Mad Enough." *New York Daily News*, September 28, 1936.

Coleman, Robert. "1938 Audience Is Akin to Dekker's 1600." *New York Daily Mirror*, January 3, 1938.

_____. "Julius Caesar." *New York Daily Mirror*, November 12, 1937.

Collins, Charles. " 'Hamlet' Comes from Dublin to Woodstock, Ill." *Chicago Sunday Tribune*, July 22, 1934.

_____. "MacLiammoir Is Exceedingly Good As Hamlet." *Chicago Tribune*, July 27, 1934.

_____. " 'Trilby' Opens Drama Season at Woodstock." *Chicago Tribune*, July 13, 1934.

Colum, Mary M. "The W.P.A. Theatre." *Forum Magazine*, February 1936.

Copland, Aaron. "Julius Caesar." *Modern Music*, November-December 1938.

"Danton's Death." *Variety*, November 9, 1938.

"The Dead Ride Fast." *Irish Times*, November 4, 1931.

"Death Takes a Holiday." *Irish Times*, January 13, 1932.

"Doctor Faustus." *Variety*, January 13, 1937.

Doyle, Peggy. " 'Five Kings' Exciting for World Premiere Audience." *Boston Evening American*, February 28, 1939.

Drake, Herbert. "The Playbill Takes to the Road." *New York Herald-Tribune*, March 26, 1939.

D. S. "Gate Theatre—A Novel Dramatized." *Irish Independent*, October 14, 1931.

_____. "Thrills in History Drama." *Irish Independent*, November 21, 1931.

Eager, Helen. "World Premiere of Orson Welles' 'Five Kings' at the Colonial." *Boston Herald*, February 28, 1939.

"Falstaff 'A Tragic Figure' in Orson Welles Production." *Christian Science Monitor*, February 17, 1939.

"Federal Project and the Devil Receive Their Due." *Newsweek*, January 23, 1937.

Gabriel, Gilbert W. "Doctor Faustus." *New York American*, January 9, 1937.

Garland, Robert. "Jazzed-Up 'Macbeth' at the Lafayette." *New York World-Telegram*, April 15, 1936.

Gassner, John W. "Too Much Good Will." *One Act Play Magazine*, January 1938.

Gilbert, Douglas. "Tragedy of 'Faustus' Ably Presented by W.P.A. Unit." *New York World-Telegram*, January 9, 1937.

Gilmore, William. "Doctor Faustus. *Brooklyn Daily Eagle*, January 9, 1937.

" 'Hamlet' at the Gate." *Irish Press*, February 3, 1932.

"Hamlet." *Irish Times*, February 3, 1932.

Hammond, Percy. "A W.P.A. 'Macbeth.' " *New York Herald-Tribune*, April 16, 1936.

_____. "Panic." *New York Herald-Tribune*, March 16, 1935.

Harkins, E. F. " 'Five Kings' Long-Winded." *Boston Daily Record*, March 1, 1939.

Hillyer, Katherine. "Orson Welles and the 'Kings' Work the Bard Overtime." *Washington Daily News*, March 14, 1939.

"Horse Eats Hat." *Brooklyn Daily Eagle*, September 28, 1936.

"Horse Eats Hat." *Nation*, October 10, 1936.

"Horse Eats Hat." *New Theatre and Film*, November 1936.

"Horse Eats Hat." *New York Sun*, September 28, 1936.

"Horse Eats Hat." *New York Times*, September 28, 1936.

"Horse Eats Hat Opens." *New York World-Telegram*, September 9, 1936.

Hughes, Elinor. " 'Five Kings' Has World Premiere at Colonial Theatre." *Boston Herald*, February 28, 1939.

Hutchens, John K. "Bard's Circus." *Boston Evening Transcript*, February 28, 1939.

Hutchens, John. " 'Five Kings' Has Boston Trial. . . ." *New York Daily News*, March 1, 1939.

Isaacs, Edith J. R. "Danton's Death." *Theatre Arts Monthly*, January 1939.

_____. "Dr. Faustus." *Theatre Arts Monthly*, March 1937.

_____. "Julius Caesar." *Theatre Arts Monthly*, January 1938.

_____. "The Shoemakers' Holiday." *Theatre Arts Monthly*, February 1938.

"Jew Suss." *Irish Times*, October 14, 1931.

" 'Jew Suss'—Romantic Drama at the Gate Theatre." *Irish Press*, October 14, 1931.

Jones, Errol Aubrey. " 'Macbeth' in Negro Background Attracts Attention to Lafayette." *New York Age*, April 25, 1936.

"Julius Caesar." *Variety*, November 17, 1937.

Keen, J. H. " 'Five Kings.' " *Philadelphia Daily News*, March 21, 1939.

Kelley, Andrew R. " 'Five Kings' Opens." *Washington Times-Herald*, March 14, 1939.

Koval, Francis. "Orson Welles." *Sight and Sound*, December 1950.

Krutch, Joseph Wood. "Benediction." *Nation*, June 11, 1938.

_____. "Better than Shakespeare?" *Nation*, May 14, 1938.

_____. "Elizabethan Frolic." *Nation*, January 15, 1938.

_____. "The Mercury Theatre." *Nation*, November 27, 1937.

_____. "Musical Cartoon." *Nation*, January 22, 1938.

Lewis, Lloyd. "The Mad Czar." *Chicago Daily News*, August 11, 1934.

_____. "Rustic Svengali." *Chicago Daily News*, July 14, 1934.

Lockridge, Richard. " 'Julius Caesar' in Modern Dress Revived by the New Mercury Theatre." *New York Sun*, November 12, 1937.

———. " 'Macbeth' with a Jungle Setting Opens at the Lafayette Theatre in Harlem." *New York Sun*, April 15, 1936.

———. "The Mercury Theatre offers a Revival of Shaw's 'Heartbreak House.' " *New York Sun*, April 30, 1938.

———. "The Mercury Theatre Presents Buchner's 'Danton's Death.' " *New York Sun*, November 3, 1938.

———. "Munitions Rocket, With Slides." *New York Sun*, October 24, 1936.

———. " 'The Shoemaker's Holiday' Makes Merry at the Mercury Theatre." *New York Sun*, January 3, 1938.

"Macbeth." *Variety*, April 22, 1936.

"Manipulating Modern Magic in 'Faustus.' " *Brooklyn Eagle*, February 21, 1937.

Manngreen. " 'Danton's Death' Scores Preview Audience." *The Daily Worker*, October 20, 1938.

Mantle, Burns. " 'Danton's Death' in the Orson Welles Manner at the Mercury." *New York Daily News*, November 3, 1938.

———. " 'Doctor Faustus' Revived by the Federal Theatre at the Maxine Elliots." *New York Daily News*, January 9, 1937.

———. " 'Heartbreak House' Revival at the Mercury is Impressive." *New York Daily News*, April 30, 1938.

———. " 'Julius Caesar' in Overcoats Mercury's First Experiment." *New York Daily News*, November 13, 1937.

———. "Mercury Revival of 'Shoemaker's Holiday' is Truly Elizabethan." *New York Daily News*, January 1, 1938.

———. "W.P.A. Black 'Macbeth' Moves from Harlem to 54th Street." *New York Daily News*, July 10, 1936.

———. "W.P.A. 'Macbeth' in Fancy Dress." *New York Daily News,* April 15, 1936.

Martin, Linton. " 'Five Kings' Opens on Chestnut Stage." *Philadelphia Inquirer*, March 21, 1939.

M. M. "Play With Thrills." *Irish Independent*, November 4, 1931.

"Mogu of the Desert." *Irish Times*, December 28, 1931.

Murdock, Henry T. " 'Five Kings' Opens at Chestnut." *Philadelphia Evening Public Ledger*, March 21, 1931.

Nathan, George Jean. "Hitler and Danton." *Newsweek*, November 14, 1938.

———. "The Mercury Climbs." *Newsweek*, January 17, 1938.

Norton, Elliot. " 'Five Kings' Stupendous Production." *Boston Post*, February 28, 1939.

Ormsbee, Helen. "Actor, Writer, Director, and Not Quite Twenty-two." *New York Herald-Tribune*, April 25, 1937.

———. "The Welles Theatre Philosophy: Everything Old Was Once New." *New York Herald-Tribune*, January 23, 1938.

"Orson Welles Says 'Five Kings' Is Return to True Shakesperean Form." *Harvard Crimson*, February 23, 1939.

Ottley, Roi. "The Negro Theatre 'Macbeth.' " *New York Amsterdam News*, April 18, 1936.

Polluck, Arthur. " 'Danton's Death' Appears at Last at the Mercury Theatre, Picturesquely Done but Whittled Down Into a Cameo." *Brooklyn Daily Eagle*, November 3, 1938.

_____. "The Federal Theater Presents 'Macbeth' in Harlem, Such a 'Macbeth' as Has Never Been Seen Before." *Brooklyn Daily Eagle*, April 16, 1936.

_____. "The Shoemaker's Holiday' Is Revived Enchantingly by the Gifted Folks of the Youthful Mercury Theater." *Brooklyn Daily Eagle*, January 1, 1938.

Schloss, Edwin H. "Orson Welles' 'Five Kings' at Chestnut." *Philadelphia Record*, March 21, 1939.

Sedgwick, Ruth Woodbury. "From A to Z." *Stage Magazine*, February 1938.

"Shakespeare Transported." *New York American*, April 16, 1936.

Sloper, L. A. " 'Five Kings' Premieres." *Christian Science Monitor*, February 28, 1939.

Thomson, Virgil. *Modern Music*, March-April 1938.

"Thriller at the Gate." *Irish Press*, November 4, 1931.

Vernon, Grenville. "Danton's Death." *Commonweal*, November 18, 1938.

_____. "Dr. Faustus." *Commonweal*, May 13, 1938.

_____. "Heartbreak House." *Commonweal*, May 13, 1938.

_____. "Julius Caesar." *Commonweal*, December 3, 1937.

_____. " 'Julius Caesar' Again." *Commonweal*, December 31, 1937.

_____. "The Shoemaker's Holiday." *Commonweal*, January 14, 1938.

Waldorf, Wilella. "Federal Project 891 of the W.P.A. Drama Forces Rejuvenates an Old French Farce with Unfortunate Results." *New York Evening Post*, September 28, 1936.

_____. "Marlowe's 'Doctor Faustus' Is Exhumed by the W.P.A." *New York Post*, January 9, 1937.

Watts, Richard, Jr. "An Event." *New York Herald-Tribune*, November 12, 1937.

_____. "Elizabethan Romp." *New York Herald-Tribune*, January 3, 1938.

_____. "Faustus." *New York Herald-Tribune*, January 9, 1936.

_____. "The Revolutionists." *New York Herald-Tribune*, November 3, 1938.

_____. "Ten Million Ghosts." *New York Herald-Tribune*, October 26, 1936.

_____. "W.P.A. Whimsy." *New York Herald-Tribune*, September 28, 1936.

Whipple, Sidney B. "Elizabethan Drama a Hit at the Mercury." *New York World-Telegram*, January 3, 1938.

_____. "New 'Julius Caesar' at Mercury Theater." *New York Sun*, November 12, 1937.

_____. "Revolution Pictured in 'Danton's Death.' " *New York World-Telegram*, November 3, 1938.

Whitman, Willson. "Uncle Sam Presents." *The Stage*, July 1936.

Winchell, Walter. "Danton's Death." *New York Daily Mirror*, November 3, 1938.

"W.P.A. Raises the Devil." *New York Sun*, January 9, 1937.

Wyatt, Euphemia Van Rensselaer. "Danton's Death." *Catholic World*, December 1938.

_____. "Friends, Romans. . . ." *Catholic World*, January 1938.

_____. "Heartbreak House." *Catholic World*, June 1938.

_____. "Labor Three Hundred Years Ago." *Catholic World*, February 1938.

_____. "The Tragical History of Doctor Faustus." *Catholic World*, February 1937.

Young, Stark. "Heartbreak House." *New Republic*, June 8, 1938.

_____. "Noctis Equi." *New Republic*, February 17, 1937.

_____. "The Mercury and London." *New Republic*, January 19, 1938.

_____. "Three Stage Versions." *New Republic*, December 1, 1937.

_____. "Two Murders: Project 891." *New Republic,* October 14, 1936.

Index

Abbey Theatre, 21-22, 27, 36
Abdul, 65
Abe Lincoln in Illinois (Sherwood), 175
Aherne, Brian, 42, 53
Allport, Gordon W., 172
American Film Institute, 53
Anderson, Arthur, 114, 115, 139, 175
Anderson, John, 121
Archduke, The (Robinson), 35
Anderson, Maxwell, 161
Anderson, Thomas, 64
"Around the World in 80 Days," 176
Ash, Walter, 144, 149, 151, 159, 161, 170
Atkinson, Brooks, 71, 121, 124

Bacon, Francis, 40
Baird, Bil, 65, 77, 82, 83, 93, 94, 102, 112
Baker, George Pierce, 27
Bankhead, Tallulah, 170
Barretts of Wimpole Street, The (Besier), 42, 43, 53
Barrymore, John, 33, 179
Beerbohm-Tree, Max, 168
Belasco, David, 66
Bell, Nelson, 160
Bengal, Ben, 104
Berstein, Dr. Maurice, 27-28, 29, 30, 31, 38
Bishop of Munster, The (Kraft), 104
Blackstone Theatre, 175
Blitzstein, Marc, 99, 101, 102, 104, 105, 114, 121, 123, 149
Bowles, Paul, 85, 86
Brecht, Bertolt, 102
Brite Lucifer (Welles), 91
Brooklyn Opera House, 42
Broun, Heywood, 116
Brown, John, 39
Brown, John Mason, 42, 71, 117, 121, 123, 133, 135, 137, 139, 153
Buchbinder, Hazel Feldman, 41
Büchner, Georg, 143, 147
Burroughs, Eric, 66, 67, 68

Candida *(Shaw), 42, 43*
Cantril, Hadley, 172, 173, 178, 179
Carnovsky, Morris, 104
Carter, Jack, 59, 62, 66, 68, 69, 95, 97, 98
Cassidy, Claudia, 47
CBS Columbia Workshop, 72
Chancellor, Betty, 35
Chimes at Midnight, 36, 170
Christophe, Henri, 56
Cinema of Orson Welles, The (Cowie), 27
Citizen Kane, 53, 55, 153, 168, 169, 171, 179
Citizen Kane Book, The (Kael), 168
Clair, Rene, 75
Clayton, John, 33, 46
Cocteau, Jean, 69
Collins, Annette, 22, 23
Collins, Ray, 175
Colonial Theater, 156
Colum, Padriac, 29
Complete Works of William Shakespeare, The, 24
Connelly, Marc, 83, 88, 170
Copland, Aaron, 100, 123
Coriolanus **(Shakespeare), 107, 112**
Cornell, Katharine, 41, 42, 43, 53
Cosgrove, Mr., 29
Cotton, Joseph, 76, 85, 87, 110, 121, 137, 144, 175
Coughlin, Father, 172-73
Coulouris, George, 113, 121, 123, 134, 142, 175
Cowie, Peter, 27, 49
Cradle Will Rock, The **(Blitzstein), 33, 99-106, 154**
Craig, Gordon, 33, 54, 117
Czar Paul **(Merejkowski), 44, 47, 49, 50.** *See also Tsar Paul*

Danton's Death (Büchner), 108, 142-54, 155, 156, 161
Danton, George Jacques, 146
Davenport, Millia, 109, 135
Dead Ride Fast, The (Sears), 35
Death Takes a Holiday **(Casella), 35**

Dekker, Thomas, 125, 127, 128, 133
Denby, Edwin, 75, 76, 77, 78, 80, 84, 85, 100
Dillinger, John, 47
Dos Passos, John, 88
Doyle, Peggy, 160
Dracula (Stoker), 90, **175**
Dr. Faustus (The Tragical History of; Marlowe, 24, 90-98, 101, 106, 108, 118, 143, 153, 156
Drunkard, The (Smith), 49
Dublin Gate Theatre, 21-22, 27, 30-36, 38, 42, 44, 49, 170

Edwards, Hilton, 21, 32, 33, 35, 36, 44, 45, 47, 49
Ellis, Maurice, 64
Emory, John, 170
Emperor Jones, The (O'Neill), 71
Engel, Lehman, 100, 123, 137
Evans, Maurice, 169
Everybody's Shakespeare, 40, 41, 113
Everyman, 24

Fairbanks, Douglas, 85
Feder, Abe, 65, 91, 93, 117, 118
Federal Theatre Project, 74, 90, 98, 99, 100, 101, 102, 104, 154, 175
"First Person Singular," 172, 173, 175
First Year, The (Craven), **124**
Five Kings, 24, 26, 53, 72, 121, 142, 149, 154 155-70
Flanagan, Hallie, 74, 101, 104
Forbes, Brenda, 43
Four Saints in Three Acts (Stein and Thomson), 53
Frankenstein (Shelley), 90
Freud, Sigmund, 14

Gabel, Martin, 88, 110, 116, 118, 121, 123, 143, 147, 166
Gabriel, Gilbert, 98
Garland, Robert, 71
Gassner, John, 126, 127, 133
Gilbert, W. S., 75
"Glass Key, The," 176
Glenavy, Lord, 32
Goodman Theatre, 24
Grapes of Wrath, The (Steinbeck), 99

Hamlet (Shakespeare), 35, 44, 47, 49, 172
Hammond, Percy, 64, 70
Harriet (Ryerson and Clements), **66**
Harvey, W. W., 56, 58

Haste to the Wedding (Gilbert), 75
Hayes, Helen, 66
Hearst, William Randolph, 14
Heartbreak House (Shaw), 15, 140
Hearts of Age, 24, 50, 51, 52
"Hell on Ice," 176
"Hell on Wheels," 175
Henry V (Shakespeare), 163, 165
(1) Henry IV (Shakespeare), 50, 163, 165
(2) Henry IV (Shakespeare), 163, 165
(3) Henry VI (Shakespeare), 24
Henry Street Playhouse, 100
Heron, Constance, 50
Herring, Clyde L., 179
Higham, Charles, 13-14
Hill, Hortense, 22, 27, 28, 30, 36, 38, 41
Hill, Noble, 22
Hill, Roger, 22, 27, 28, 30, 31, 36, 38, 39, 40, 41, 42, 43, 44, 45, 46, 49, 73, 141
Hitler, Adolf, 106, 109, 147, 176
Holinshed's Chronicles, 163
Holland, Joseph, 106, 109, 110, 111, 112, 121
Horse Eats Hat (Denby and Welles), 74-89, 101, 143, 156
Horton, Asadata Dafora, 65
Houseman, John, 24, 53, 54, 56, 71, 72, 74, 77, 95, 99, 100, 101, 102, 104, 107, 117, 118, 120, 134, 142, 143, 149, 154, 155, 156, 157, 159, 169, 171, 172, 173, 175
Hoyt, John, 43, 45
Hulett, Otto, 89
Huston, John, 175
Hutchens, John K., 159

Importance of Being Earnest, The (Wilde), 142
Irving, Henry, 168
Isaacs, Edith, 95, 98
Italian Straw Hat, An (Labiche), **74, 75, 84**

Jane Eyre, 175
Jerome, V. J., 101, 149-50
Jew Süss (Feuchtwanger), **31, 32, 33, 34, 35, 42**
Jones, Errol Aubrey, 70
Jordan, Joe, 69
Julius Caeser (Shakespeare), 25, 40, 53, 68, 72, 106-23, 124, 125, 133, 134, 135, 139, 142, 143, 146, 148, 151, 153, 156, 159, 160, 169, 175

Kael, Pauline, 168, 169
Kane, Whitford, 45, 46, 134, 142
Karson, Nat, 57, 64, 68, 85
Kaye, Henriette, 87
Keen, J. H., 160

Kerr, Walter, 121
King, Carol, 78
Kingsley, Sidney, 89
Koch, Howard, 175, 176, 179
Kraft, H. S., 104
Krutch, Joseph Wood, 88, 114, 117

Labiche, Eugene, 75, 76, 84
Lafayette Theatre, 54, 58, 66
Langner, Lawrence, 157
Lanner, Josef, 61, 69
Laurel, Stan, 139
Lee, Canada, 66
Les Miserables, 172
Leve, Samuel, 68, 118, 119, 120, 134, 136
Lewis, Lloyd, 47
Lloyd, Harold, 79
Lloyd, Norman, 55, 106, 111, 114, 115, 135, 137, 142
Lockridge, Richard, 71, 149
Lonely Man, The (Koch), 175
Longford, Lord, 32, 42
Long, Huey, 172, 73
Lulubelle (Belasco), 66

Macbeth (Shakespeare), 41, 74, 85, 107, 159, 172
McBride, Joseph, 27
McClintic, Guthrie, 42, 43
MacGowan, Kenneth, 38
McKee, Harry, 92
MacLeish, Archibald, 53, 99, 101, 171
MacLiammoir, Michael, 21, 32, 33, 35, 36, 44, 45, 47, 49
Macy, Gertrude, 42
Magic Curtain, The (Langner), 157
Magnificent Ambersons, The, 179
Mankiewicz, Herman, 55
Mantle, Burns, 71, 127
Marc-Michel, 75
"March of Time, The," 171, 172
Marching Song (Welles and Hill), 40
Marford, Charles, 33
Marlowe, Christopher, 91, 94, 95, 98, 120, 143
Marx Brothers, 78, 79
Maxine Elliott Theatre, 74, 93, 101, 102
Merchant of Venice, The (Shakespeare), 40, 41
Mercury Shakespeare, The, 41, 73
Mercury Theatre, 24, 31, 53, 54, 99, 104, 106, 108, 109, 113, 117, 118, 120, 123, 125, 127, 133, 140, 142, 143, 144, 151, 153, 154, 155, 156, 157, 159, 172, 175
Mercury-Theatre Guild, 26

"Mercury Theatre on the Air," 38, 174, 175, 176, 179
Meredith, Burgess, 161
Merry Wives of Windsor, The (Shakespeare), 11
Mogu of the Desert (Column), 35
Molière (Jean-Baptiste Poquelin), 24
Morcum, James, 144, 158, 164, 166
Morehead, Agnes, 175
Morrow, Irving, 42
Murdock, Henry, 161
Murrow, Edward R., 70
Mussolini, Benito, 106, 107, 109

Nathan, George Jean, 125-26, 127
New Theatre League, 104
Nicholson, Leo, 50
Nicholson, Virginia, 50, 53, 56, 68, 117, 145, 172, 175. *See also* Pringle, Virginia; Welles, Virginia

O'Brien, Richard, 173
O'Callaigh, Cathral, 32
O'Connaire, Issac, 29
Offenbach, Jacques, 85
O'Neil, Charles, 49
Othello (Shakespeare), 36
Otley, Roi, 70
Our Town (Wilder), 82

Panic (MacLeish), 53, 171
Paramount Theatre, 94
Paul, Edgerton, 24, 52
Peacock Theatre, 36, 37
Physician in Spite of Himself, The (Molière), 24
Pirandello, Luigi, 82
Plant in the Sun (Bengal), 104
Playwright's Company, 175
Polluck, Arthur, 71
Porgy and Bess (Heyward and Gershwin), 66
Price, Vincent, 142
Pringle, Virginia, 50, 53, 56, 68, 117, 145, 172, 175. *See also* Nicholson, Virginia; Welles, Virginia
Project 891, 74, 94
Prussing, Lois, 49

Raquello, Ramon, 177
Raynor, Henry, 73
Reddin, Norman, 32
Reinhardt, Max, 85, 117, 143
Reis, Irving, 114
Richard III (Shakespeare), 24
Richard II (Shakespeare), 163

Rise and Fall of the City of Mahagonny, The (Brecht and Weill), 102
Robespierre, Maximilian, 146
Romeo and Juliet (Shakespeare), 42, 43 72
Rosenthal, Jean, 112, 118, 120, 134, 149, 157
Rossiter, A. P., 24
Run-Through (Houseman), 15, 118, 155

St. James Theatre, 89
Satie, Erik, 85
Saunders, Wardell, 64, 68
Schiller, Friedrich, 85
Schilling, Gus, 162
Sears, David, 35
Second Hurricane, The (Copland and Denby), 100
"Seventeen," 176
Shadow, The, 114
Shakespeare, William, 24, 40, 55, 56, 58, 60-61, 63, 69, 70, 71, 72, 90, 106, 107, 108, 109, 117, 120, 127, 143, 153, 159, 160, 161, 163, 168, 169
Sherman, Hiram, 46, 68, 72, 77, 94, 95, 111, 118, 121, 125, 135, 137, 138, 139, 142
Sherwood, Robert 175
Shoemaker's Holiday, The (Dekker), 68, 108, 118, 124-41, 142, 151, 169
Shruers, Edward, 102, 103
Shubert Organization, 74
Sight and Sound, 73
Six Characters in Search of an Author (Pirandello), 82
Sketches of Hayti (Harvey), 56
Sokoloff, Vladimir, 147
Speaight, Robert, 160
Spencer, Arthur, 92
Stalin, Joseph, 148, 149, 151
Stein, Gertrude, 53
Stevens, Ashton, 46
Stewart, Paul, 175

Tchaikowsky, Peter, 175
Teichmann, Howard, 176
Ten Million Ghosts (Kingsley), 89
Theatre Guild, The, 21, 32, 104, 154, 155, 156, 157, 159, 169, 179
Thomas, Edna, 59, 65, 66, 68, 69, 72

Thomson, Virgil, 53, 61, 69, 75, 85, 86, 123
Tichacek, Jan, 150
Todd, Richard Kimble, 22
Too Much Johnson (Gillette), 15, 121, 142, 144, 145
"Treasure Island," 175
Trilby (DeMaurier and Potter), 47, 48
Trotsky, Leon, 148, 149, 151
Tsar Paul (Merejkowski), 44, 47, 49, 50. *See also Czar Paul*
Twelfth Night (Shakespeare), 38, 39, 40

Vance, Bill, 50, 53
Van Gogh, Vincent, 175
van Witsen, Leo, 152
Venice Theatre, 102
Vernon, Grenville, 114, 116, 117, 121
"Voodo" Macbeth, 53, 54-73, 88, 101, 120, 156, 169, 172

Waldorf, Wilella, 94, 95
"War of the Worlds," 53, 154, 171, 173, 176, 177, 178, 179
Warring-Manley, Marian, 134
Warshow, Robert, 99
Watts, Richard, 139, 153
Webster, Margaret, 169
Wedding March, The (Gilbert), 75
Weill, Kurt, 102
Welles, Richard, 22, 76
Welles, Virginia, 50, 53, 56, 68, 117, 145, 172, 175. *See also* Nicholson, Virginia; Pringle, Virginia
Whipple, Sidney, 127
Whitman, Willson, 70
Wilder, Thorton, 42, 82
Wilson, Richard, 151
Winter of Discontent (Shakespeare and Welles), 24, 26
Winterset (Anderson), 161
Woollcot, Alexander, 42
W.P.A., 24, 53, 64, 66, 69, 70, 74, 77, 82, 101, 175
W.P.A. Negro Theatre Project, 54, 66, 69, 70, 72, 74
Wyatt, Eustace, 148, 175

Young, Stark, 93, 95, 98, 112, 114, 116, 117

Orson Welles has been hailed as one of the most brilliant actors and directors in the history of the cinema and the theatre, and although Welles's film career has been examined and reexamined in print for years, almost no attention has been paid to his relatively short, yet nevertheless meteoric, career in the world of the stage. In this critical biography of that portion of Welles's artistic endeavors, Dr. France tells how Welles functioned dynamically in that world—how, in the space of four years, he conceived several of the most celebrated and ambitious productions in the history of the American stage. And all this *before* he turned twenty-five!

The Theatre of Orson Welles begins with Welles's student acting and directing experiences at the Todd School for Boys in Woodstock, Illinois, moves to his professional debut as an actor with the Dublin Gate Theatre at the advanced age of sixteen, follows him back to America for summer stock in Illinois, recounts in detail his major productions in New York under the auspices of the WPA and his own Mercury Theatre enterprise, covers his ground-breaking work in radio, including his famous *War of the Worlds* broadcast, and concludes with his departure for Hollywood to make *Citizen Kane*. Two helpful ap-